A Way of Working

A Way of Working

Edited by D. M. Dooling

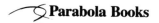

Parabola Books

Parabola Books
656 Broadway
New York, NY 10012-2317

Parabola Books are published by the Society for the Study of Myth and Tradition, a nonprofit organization devoted to the dissemination and exploration of materials relating to myth, symbol, ritual, and art of the great religious traditions. The Society also publishes PARABOLA, The Magazine of Myth and Tradition.

Grateful acknowledgment is made for permission to reprint the following 62 excerpts:

"The Props assist the House," by Emily Dickinson, from *The Complete Poems of Emily Dickinson*, edited by Thomas H. Johnson. Copyright 1914, 1942 by Martha Dickinson Bianchi, by permission of Little, Brown and Co. Lines 4 and 5 of the same poem reprinted by permission of the publishers and the Trustees of Amherst College from *The Poems of Emily Dickinson*, edited by Thomas H. Johnson, Cambridge, Mass.: The Belknap Press of Harvard University Press. Copyright 1951, © 1955 by the President and Fellows of Harvard College.

"The Joiner," from *Her-Bak Chick-Pea: The Living Face of Ancient Egypt.* Copyright 1954 by Isha Schwaller de Lubicz and © 1955 by Ernest Flammarion, published by and with the permission of Inner Traditions International, New York.

"Prince Hui's Excellent Cook," from *The Bible of the World*, edited by Robert O. Ballou. Copyright 1939 by Robert O. Ballou, copyright © 1967 by Robert O. Ballou. All Rights Reserved. Reprinted by permission of Viking Penguin Inc.

"The Hose-maker" and "The Parable of the Wood-cutter," from *Tales of the Hasidim, The Early Masters,* by Martin Buber. Copyright 1947 by Schocken Books Inc. Copyright renewed © 1975 by Schocken Books Inc.

"Duke Hwan and the Wheelwright," from *The Way of Chuang Tzü*, by Thomas Merton. Copyright © 1965 by The Abbey of Gethsemani. Reprinted by permission of New Directions Publishing Corporation.

ISBN: 0-930407-01-6
Library of Congress Catalog Card Number: 78-68366

Printed in the United States of America

Second Printing 1987

CONTENTS

INTRODUCTION

"Man's activity consists in either a making or a doing," writes A. K. Coomaraswamy in *Christian and Oriental Philosophy of Art*. "Both of these aspects of the active life depend for their correction on the contemplative life."[1]

In this book we are considering craft as the paradigm of man's total activity—a making, a doing, and an act of contemplation—as it refers to man the maker, man the user, and man the tool, man the receiver and transmitter of forces of creation much greater than himself. We are looking at craft as a model of a complex of relationships with "above" and "below," an image of human functioning and so of man, who is the traditional bridge between God and animal, between heaven and earth. We are looking at craft as a way in which a man may create and cross a bridge in himself and center himself in his own essential unity.

Crossing a bridge, there is passage in both directions: from "above" to "below," whether by divine revelation, as the myths tell us, or from transmitted knowledge, the Idea incorporated in concrete form; and from "below" to "above," the transformation of raw material into useful beauty. From the interaction of these two movements comes the transformation of him in whom they meet and relate.

We wish to re-examine the traditional view of the sacred nature of craft as the symbol of man's potential wholeness, as well as his way toward that wholeness. Once there was no divorce between art and craft; in medieval society, painters and sculptors as well as potters and weavers were members of craft guilds. A man *was* a carpenter, a painter, or a stonemason; his work, his way of life, was central to his identity and recognized as his means of centering and discovering himself. It was holy; it was his "religion," his relinking with his divine source. This is far from the modern view, and if in this book we speak of "craft" as "the making of beautiful things for use" and turn our attention to wood and stone and clay and wool, we by no means limit craft to these samples. Rather, we see it as an essential element of "work"—indeed, of the whole functioning of man, for we are taking craft as the pattern of all of a man's manifestations. What we see here is equally applicable to all the rest: the workings of the invisible material of thought and feeling in all his modes of expressing himself, in all his arts, in all his work, and in his human relationships.

In spite of the divorce that seems to have taken place in our times, craft cannot be separated from art any more than usefulness can be separated from beauty. The word "art" comes from an Indo-European root meaning "to fit together," from which also comes "order," which began as a word meaning a row of threads on a loom. "Craft" originally meant "strength, skill, device," indicating at its very inception the basic relationships of the material, the maker, and the tool: the opposition of thrust and resistance and the means of their coming together in a creative reconciliation. The artist must be a craftsman, for without the working knowledge of this triple relationship subject to opposing forces, he has not the skill to express his vision. And if the craftsman has no contact with the "Idea," which is the vision of the artist, he is at best a competent manufacturer. Art and craft are aspects (potential, not guaranteed) of all work that is undertaken intentionally and voluntarily; all work, in other words, that is worthily human, that is not "donkey work" or drudgery, the labor of an animal or a machine. Both art and craft must take part in any activity which has the power to transform.

In the three-way relationship of maker, material, and tool in this evolutionary process, the tool also is a symbol that demands a respectful approach, for it is not every chisel that can transmit truth, and not every potter is a transformed being. The traditional concept of craft as a link between contemplation and action, at the service of life as well as an expression of a divine revelation, is hardly a common idea in our present world. The emphasis is on the production of objects rather than on the self-creation of the artisan and the development of his total consciousness. This is the inevitable exteriorization which takes place as action moves away from knowledge. It is not considered that the material can or should modify the craftsman, only vice versa; or, least of all, that the user of the crafted object—the "consumer"—has in his way of using it the smallest responsibility to a whole possible process of creation. As Coomaraswamy points out, we suffer no qualms of conscience and would not dream of qualifying it as a destructive act when we convert a ritual instrument or a sacred image into a mantelpiece ornament. We use the word "creative" with increasing frequency and less and less rigor in its definition.

Except in rare and isolated areas, crafts no longer exist as a way of life. The "liberation of the man with the hoe" that took place in the last century removed the possibilities for the enrichment of society contained in manual work, along with the abuses that had collected around it. In our day, crafts are newly respectable, but chiefly as "hobbies," as "occupational therapy," or as new fashions in interior decorating. Yet behind the excuses given for indulging in craft activities, there lurks a kind of half-buried question, a faint suspicion that there is more to all this. Why is the attraction so strong, why is one alternately so energized and so baffled by this new pastime?

If we would rediscover the meaning that crafts had in medieval society—the living social structure of the guilds, the initiatory sense of art and of work—we need to look for the laws of a kind of creation that we talk about, perhaps too easily. What is it that makes a crafted object true art, that gives it more than physical beauty and usefulness, that makes it a communication bringing about a change in both the giver and the receiver of the message? Where does the possibility lie of a passage of living forces, of a veritable creation? Is it the artisan who creates? Where does the process begin?

The myths and the traditions tell us that it begins from above; that all art, all craft, starts as a divine revelation. "Ideas," writes Coomaraswamy, "are gifts of the spirit, and not to be confused with talents; ideas are never made, but can only be 'invented,' that is, 'found' and entertained . . . Before the artist can even imagine a form there must have been a direction of the will towards a specific idea." "Inspiration" means infusion with the spirit or breath of the divine; the "enthusiast" is god-possessed. The craftsman's search is first to be open to receive this breath, this word; then, with the help of his craft-skill, to be at its service, in order that it may be expressed: conceived and reborn. This imitation and re-expression is not just a representation or symbolic act, but an actual rearrangement of the flow and order of energy. From the same word which is the root of "art" and "order" comes the carpenter's word for "joinery" in Greek, *harmos,* from which comes "harmony." This process of rearrangement, this change, operates on the craftsman also; his material modifies him as he modifies it, in proportion to his openness, his awareness of the exchange that is taking place. And the results, in terms of art, clearly visible to the beholder, are also proportional. Conscious art—and "mechanical" or "accidental" art is a contradiction in terms; as

Plato says, "We cannot give the name of art to anything irra-
tional"—depends on the presence of the artisan; and he is
present, he himself is there with what he uniquely is, only in
such a state of whole awareness. Nothing that is machine-made,
whether by mass production in a factory or by an unconscious
and mechanical workman, can be a channel for that direct, living exchange which is experienced, however rarely, in the sight
and touch of certain handmade objects, when a palpable energy
is transmitted, something of life itself.

So if we dare use the word "creative," we must see that its
possibility lies in that mysterious human property of attentiveness: not a merely mental attention, but an attention which
relates and mobilizes the sensitive intelligence of the body, the
affective intelligence of the feeling, and the ordering intelligence
of the mind toward a more total openness to what is: a fact, a
truth, "found" or revealed, and the real life, the living energy,
which that contains. Neither the fact to be restated nor the
technique for doing so belongs to the craftsman, nor is he the
creator of either. "The craftsman in primitive societies never
imagined himself to be doing the work himself," M. L. von
Franz tells us in her book on creation myths. "Nowadays if
you watch a carpenter or a smith . . . he feels that his skill is a
man-made possession, which he owns. If we look at the folk-
lore and mythology of the different crafts in more primitive
societies, we see that they have a much more adequate view of
it. They all still have tales which show that man never invented
any craft or skill, but that it was *revealed* to him, that it is the
Gods who produced the knowledge which man now uses if he
does anything practical."[2]

What, then, *is* the creation of the craftsman? If he is not the
owner but the servant of his concept, if he recognizes himself as
the receiver rather than the author of the message, he also sees
that this concept, this message, depends on him for a new form
through which it can be transmitted. He is called to its service,

he is vital to it: the words will not be heard unless he can
rephrase them, give them a new sound; but the message itself is
not his to change. So the member of a guild did not sign his
work, and if he worked alone, it was for the convenience of the
task, not for personal credit. Crafts are traditionally anony-
mous and communal, coming from the hierarchy of the guilds
—"our" work and not "my" work—the work of relationship
and of faithfulness to a whole that is greater than the person.
And here, of course, is the authenticity and the dimension of
real art, true craft: on another level from that of the individual
and his identification with the result of "his" work. It is only if
the individual can submit to a larger authority, in order to take
part in it, that craft can serve creatively both art and the artisan.

This purpose has never been more important than at the
present time. For as Coomaraswamy tells us, what has been
preserved and transmitted in crafts, in simple folk art, is "a
series of what are really esoteric doctrines and symbols of anything but popular invention. One may say that it is in this way,
when an intellectual decadence has taken place in higher cir-
cles, that this doctrinal material is preserved from one epoch to
another, affording a glimmer of light in what may be called the
dark night of the intellect; the folk memory serving the purpose
of a sort of ark, in which the wisdom of the former age is
carried over the period of the dissolution of cultures that takes
place at the close of the cycle."[3]

This book was written by a group of people who came together because of a shared interest in the possibility that crafts
might indeed be a "sort of ark" for the transmission of real
knowledge about being. We are not "craftsmen" in the accepted sense of the word, but most of us are involved in one
way or another with writing. We agreed, theoretically, that the
laws of the craft process were applicable to any activity; but in

practice, how did they apply to thinking and to writing? We asked ourselves if it would be possible to write a book together —not just a collection of essays, but a book developing a single line of thought. We wanted to experience what we could of the craft process by sharing an effort, by working together in a way that we felt must have been an important element in the strength of the traditional guilds. So, as if we were companions in such a guild, we undertook, as a task in common, the planning, execution, and putting together of our varying materials. The result for us is the change we have experienced in our materials and our understanding and the fact that the questions with which we began are clearer.

And the master craftsman to whom we looked for guidance?

Once, Chuang Tzü tells us, there was a master craftsman who made such beautiful things out of wood that the King himself demanded to know the secret of his art.

"Your Highness," said the carpenter, "there is no secret; but there is something. This is how I begin:

"When I am about to make a table, I first collect my energies and bring my mind to absolute quietness.

"I become oblivious of any reward to be gained or any fame to be acquired. When I am free from the influences of all such outer considerations, I can listen to the inner voice which tells me clearly what I have to do.

"When my skill is thus concentrated, I take up my ax; I make sure that it is perfectly sharp, that it fits my hand and swings with my arm. Then I enter the forest.

"I look for the right tree: the tree that is waiting to become my table. And when I find it, I ask: 'What have I for you, and what have you for me?'

"Then I cut down the tree and set to work.

"I remember how my masters taught me to bring my skill

and my thought into relation with the natural qualities of the wood."

The King said, "When the table is finished, it has a magical effect upon me; I cannot treat it as I would any other table.

"What is the nature of this magic?"

"Your Majesty," said the carpenter, "what you call magic comes only from what I have already told you."

A Way of Working

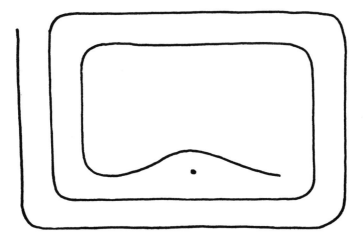

"Your Highness," said the carpenter, "there is no secret; but there is something. This is how I begin."

I: *FREE TIME*

Our stories say that once before time—our time—began, spring was the only season. Earth, our greathearted and unstinting mother, supplied us with all things needful. Days were sunny, evenings cool, the lion lay with the lamb. Unprompted by hoe or plowshare, fields broke spontaneously into amber waves of richly tasseled maize; mushrooms and strawberries abounded in the spacious woods, oaks groaned with the health-giving acorn. The rivers ran with nectar. At the heart of it all our first parents had dominion and kept a fabulous garden.

The thought of them stirs us still. What did they look like, newly made with all that free time in consumers' paradise, in that deathless, prenatal world our stories conjure? We call them "happy" but what can such a word signify applied to such persons in such a place? And what on earth did they do? "Not to irksome toil but to delight He made us," Milton conceives of Adam saying, and something wistful in us sighs assent and drowns in paradox. "Happy work," alas, is hardly work at all but play or recreation. Work is out of place in Eden. Or in any case, such tending and keeping, such lopping and pruning as we dream of in that enchanted plantation discovered in full bloom upon awakening must be understood as some sort of ritual or symbolic gesture—*noblesse oblige*—since in the nature of things it was not required for survival; it had no ecological function. For the rest they christened the birds and beasts and "had dominion" over every living thing.

In fact, before they fall into time and the only world we know, Adam and Eve are radiant enigmas: they lack feature and certifiable character. Indeed our stories have neither point nor plot until we recollect who tells them, and why—they are a measure of our discontent with what we are and how we live. The garden of delight grows out of our cursed, irksome ground, thick with weeds and thistles. The meaning of perpetual spring is that we are cold and tired. The man with the hoe, sweat on his brow, pictures a paradise of free time: the bright blank faces of Eve and Adam beguile his weariness. In an iron age we dream of gold.

Experience cannot imagine innocence except to say, deeply stirred, that it is infinitely precious and doomed. Adam and Eve are not *our* parents at all until the serpent stirs and they eat and hide and in the cool of the day the Lord walks one last time in the garden. It is time for time—*our* time—to begin. Our stories render the words of the second and final creation as: "In the sweat of thy face shalt thou eat bread, till thou return unto the ground; for out of it wast thou taken: for dust thou art, and unto dust shalt thou return."

In the garden, conditions were such that time was suspended, reward was immediate—there for the picking—and work as we know it did not exist. When the Lord later lifted his curse from the ground and made an everlasting covenant with Noah he did not—that is to say, we cannot imagine that he could—undo or resuspend the condition of time. Eden cannot exist if, as the Lord says, "While the earth remaineth, seedtime and harvest, and cold and heat, and summer and winter, and day and night shall not cease." This age is iron: you must work or starve.

And work so regarded is one key consequence of what our stories call "the fall."

Yet even within a fallen—that is to say, an historical—world, our stories seek out comforting exceptions: the simple life for example (the noble savage, the Sicilian shepherd with his flute, a home on the range, the village blacksmith), or golden ages of faith and faithful labor. In *The Need for Roots* Simone Weil is moved by what she judges to be traces of such times:

> There are numerous signs indicating . . . that long ago physical labor was preeminently a religious activity and consequently something sacred. The Mysteries—a religion that embraced the whole of pre-Roman antiquity—were entirely founded upon symbolical expressions concerning the salvation of the soul, drawn from agriculture. The same symbolism is found again in the New Testament parables . . . There may perhaps have been a time when an identical truth was translated into different sets of symbols, and when each set was adapted to a certain type of physical labor in such a way as to turn the latter into a direct expression of religious faith.[1]

The myth of an age of faith, an age in which working is praying (*laborare est orare* is the old monkish phrase), is particularly poignant in times like our own. An age of faith would mean an age in which many of us could truly accept the living authority of the sacred in the world and in time and could wholeheartedly acknowledge that our relation to that presence was the single most vital relation in all our mortal lives. An age of faith might well imply a golden age of work since in such an age every act or gesture, no matter how secret or servile or burdensome, no matter how worldly or unworldly its context, would have *also* inhering in it a ceremonial function attesting to the individual worker's willing, more or less conscious relation to the sacred. A hundred years ago the priest and poet Gerard Manley Hopkins—who did not live in such an age—meditated from the pulpit on the theme of *laborare est orare*:

> It is not only prayer that gives God glory but work. Smiting on an anvil, sawing a beam, whitewashing a wall, driving horses, sweeping, scouring, everything gives God some glory if being in His Grace you do it as your duty . . . To lift up the hands in prayer gives God glory, but a man with a dungfork in his hand, a woman with a slop pail, give Him glory too. He is so great that all things give Him glory if you mean they should.[2]

In an age of faith my work, that old hard sentence I labor out in the sweat of my face until the day I die, would be transformed into a duty owed to what I know I have most at heart. If I faltered, I would be surrounded and steadied by my brothers and sisters in God. Faith can move mountains by quarrying them and, as this witness by the Archbishop of Rouen shows (as cited by the historian Henry Adams), by bearing them miles over the plain to the village of Chartres.

> Who has ever seen! Who has ever heard tell, in times past, that powerful princes of the world, that men brought up in honour and in wealth, that nobles, men and women, have bent their proud and haughty necks to the harness of carts, and that, like beasts of burden, they have dragged to the abode of Christ these waggons, loaded with wines, grains, oil, stone, wood, and all that was necessary for the wants of life, or for the reconstruction of the church? . . . When they halt on the road, nothing is heard but the confession of sins, and pure and suppliant prayer to God to obtain pardon. At the voice of the priests who exhort their hearts to peace, they forget all hatred, discord is thrown far aside, debts are remitted, the unity of hearts is established . . . When

they have reached the church they arrange the waggons about it like a spiritual camp, and during the whole night they celebrate the watch by hymns and canticles.[3]

Such an age seems very far away. The medievalism of Hopkins' fellow—and non-Catholic—Victorians, such as Carlyle or Ruskin or Morris (or, in America, someone like Henry Adams), is very much an index of discontent with the signs of their own secular times (which are also ours) and, as such, more of a poem of longing than objective history. For Adams the sacred presence of the Virgin at Chartres some six hundred years ago had "acted as the greatest force the Western world [had] ever felt,"[4] and standing before the giant dynamo in the Gallery of Machines at the Paris Exposition of 1900 he could only be ruefully aware that there was no power in the modern world which could, like the Virgin, raise Chartres. And three quarters of a century later, with the energy of the split atom added to our means, we most likely agree.

We agree and at the same time recognize that an age of faith is not among our present options. If I had what William Butler Yeats called medieval knees I might well bow to the glorious yoke more willingly, but I am stuck with the stiff joints I have. To the infidel suspicious of his own nostalgia, even the old testimonies are suspect. What percentage of the cathedral builders, for instance, were assigned to the carving of those marvelous gargoyles about which Ruskin writes so eloquently? How many workmen got to grind and measure out the famous sapphire dust that gave those windows their heavenly blue? Labor was labor even in the middle ages, the infidel surmises, and most of our ancestors were not craftsmen but oxen and asses, not carvers but stonebreakers and haulers. Even the good Archbishop of Rouen seems primarily dazzled by the unique spectacle of *noblemen* drawing those laden carts and performing—for a limited period only, it must be remembered—serfs'

work. But what about the serfs themselves who did this for
their living? Were they blessed in their work? Not even Henry
Adams can say; they could not write and left no diaries.

Still, standing in the presence of their surviving structures—
not the cathedrals of Europe only, but the great heads of Easter
Island, the pyramids of Mexico and Egypt, Stonehenge, the
Parthenon, the "Wailing Wall"—something strange can hap-
pen. The stones speak an unfamiliar language that can touch
us. Afterward we muse upon ages of faith and a mysterious
way of working that would transform the worker as well as the
work—upon a relation to a sacred authority lost, then dimly
apprehended, now lost again. Our persisting and lovable stories
tell the truth about *us,* at least: that we feel ourselves out of
phase and inharmonious, lacking a center within and without;
that even infidels feel a need for something sacred in their lives;
that what we do for our living—our work—ought somehow to
dignify, perhaps glorify, certainly not mock, that living.

The Concise Oxford Dictionary defines "work" as "an expenditure of energy, striving, application of effort to some purpose." For many, the purpose is subsistence or livelihood; short
of starving we have no alternative—we work to subsist and
such work is the price we pay, penal in nature, a necessary evil.
Thus *ponos,* Greek for "work," has the same root as the Latin
poena: "punishment," "penalty," "pain." Thus Karl Marx
sees work as typically "an alienation of life since . . . I work in
order to [provide] for myself the means of living. Working is
not living."[5] Particularly since the Industrial Revolution and
the coming of what Carlyle calls the Age of Machinery, work
has seemed sterile and self-estranging. "The shuttle drops from
the fingers of the weaver," he writes in "Signs of the Times"
(1829), "and falls into iron fingers that ply it faster . . . Not
the external and physical alone is now managed by machinery,
but the internal and spiritual also." The French writer Simone
Weil, speaking out of her brief but crucial experience on the as-

sembly line at the Renault works in the 1930s, saw such work as meaning for most "a daily death": "To labor is to place one's own being, body and soul, in the circuit of inert matter, turn it into an intermediary between one state and another of a fragment of matter, to make of it an instrument . . . an appendage of the tool."[6]

For more fortunate others, on the other hand, work may be said to pay: that is, by means of my work I am able to buy free time, time during which I may do as I please. In such cases I sleep until noon, read *Paradise Lost,* do needlepoint, or fly south for the weekend, feeling my work was worth it. Here work is regarded as a currency, a means of exchange, and its value lies principally in what it is able to purchase above and beyond subsistence. The end consoles us for the means and *the end will always involve not working.* As Alasdair Clayre writes, "Work may be done without effort or reward; but what is done consistently without either tends to be called something else—a game or a hobby."[7] Or, nowadays, a "craft."*

St. Luke tells of two sisters, Mary and Martha, who receive the ministering Jesus in their home, along with his disciples and followers. But while Mary sits with the rest at the feet of the master, attentive to his word, Martha finds herself preparing and serving the meal for them all. And when at length her bitterness lends her courage and she complains to her chief guest of her sister's leaving her to drudge alone and asks him to bid Mary help her, she is gently but firmly reproved: "Martha,

---

* Jean-Jacques Rousseau recommends the way of the craftsman as the best of all ways of earning one's livelihood. But a craft for Rousseau is not regarded as a value in and of itself: it is a method of purchasing time and economic independence through a minimal expenditure of energy. In his ideological novel *Émile,* for example, Rousseau has his young hero learn a craft—carpentry in this case—on the grounds that it is "a purely mechanical skill where the hands work more than the head, and which does not lead to a fortune, but on which one can manage to live." For Rousseau a craft is a work condition that frees us from society and *makes fewer demands on us than usual.* It is good less for what it is than for what it isn't.

Martha, thou art careful and troubled about many things: But one thing is needful: and Mary hath chosen that good part, which shall not be taken away from her."

How is one to understand this? Certainly there is a parallel with the earlier lesson of the loaves and fishes, when troubled disciples feared there was not enough food to feed the assembled multitude and a miracle proved their fears unfounded. In the sermon on the mountain we are urged to take no thought for food or drink and the priorities are clearly stated: "Seek ye first the kingdom of God, and his righteousness; and all these things shall be added unto you." So Mary has chosen the "needful" part: nourishing the understanding through an act of self-quieting and attention (if thus we might interpret her sitting at his feet and hearing his word) is a more urgent human concern than administering to the needs of the flesh. Or one might read this episode with the maxim *laborare est orare* in mind: the way of active service is as much a prayer, a turning toward the sacred, as is the way of contemplation or abstention from action. In this case Martha is rebuked for failing to see the potentialities of her own part and coveting another's.

And yet . . . the infidel's heart, troubled, goes out to Martha. The kitchen door swings shut but not before she has caught a last glimpse of her sister settling herself to listen. The bread needs slicing and the knife is dull. On no account must she rattle the plates and already she can catch—if she holds her breath and strains—the sound of his voice though not the words. And if Mary chose to stay and listen to them, Martha is here by default; she has no choice. If she does not serve, the guests will not be fed and the laws of hospitality are mocked. It is bitter. Her faith is not confident. She is not free to do what she would choose to do. Full of cares, she feels she lacks free time. And it is bitterer still when he turns to her with his look and says, "Martha, Martha, thou art careful and troubled about many things . . ."

"Our age," wrote Simone Weil just before her death in 1943, "has as its own particular mission, or vocation, the creation of a civilization founded upon the spiritual nature of work."[8] In the chapters to follow we try to explore the possibilities of such a creation, for ourselves if not for the age at large, amounting to an alternative understanding of, and means of participation in, the human condition of work. "A way of working" is one way of putting it. And the troubled and troubling presence of our sister Martha should never be forgotten. This chapter, at least, is dedicated to her.

"When I am about to make a table, I first collect my energies and bring my mind to absolute quietness."

II: *FREE SPACE*

As Martha recrosses the threshold into the kitchen, what is she thinking? The words of apparent reproval sting, and there is more than a touch of resentment in her. Now, to all her troubles and concerns is added the turmoil of doubts and questions. Among them, one is uppermost: "But one thing is needed"— and what is that? What one thing is necessary, among ten thousand things all claiming necessity, all demanding one's attention? Should she turn back and try to imitate Mary? Should she just forget about the words of Christ and prepare dinner? What should she do? What is expected? How should she be? The words have touched a nerve, have awakened a longing so profound that her wish to listen, to hear and ponder, has risen and become uppermost. But how can she drop everything that must be done for the comfort of her guests and still remain herself? Mary has chosen the better part, but has Martha chosen hers? Or is she in that limbo between wanting and not wanting, between yes and no? It is Mary's nature, perhaps, to listen, to be always among the disciples, and Martha's to work, to prepare the meal, to serve. And yet for Martha another need is there, too: the need to hear, to learn, to receive the teaching.

Two possibilities appear: to shut the door and go about the

business of preparing the meal, forgetting that other need; or, if possible, to *include* that need along with her essential nature: to work, prepare, and serve. But something still is necessary if one is to do both at once, and as Martha returns to the kitchen, she is in despair, not knowing how to be at once disciple and cook.

She sees, as she enters the doorway, the cake waiting to go into the oven, the knives and bowls that are her tools. She has turned from one demand only to find another. To turn back now, to sit with Mary among the others—that is not possible, for the concerns and troubles would only reappear and intrude themselves upon her attention, and again the words would be lost. But to turn away from the words, back to the clutter and clatter of the kitchen, seems impossible too. Her body is heavy with fatigue; she closes her eyes, and for a moment Martha the capable yields humbly to incapacity. In that instant something in her opens, and there comes a moment of pause, of stillness. Free time appears. She is now both Martha and Mary: but until now, how much of either has she been? She is in charge of the household, but she sees now that her usual attitude is to be troubled and concerned as if she did not know how to do all the countless things that need doing. But she does know: her hands know the making of bread, the mixing and carving and tasting that is the cook's business. Her eyes miss nothing that is out of place, and the sweeping and cleaning do not need the energy of worry. She opens her eyes, and she sees that with free time there is free space too, within and without. A new energy takes shape in her body, an energy that knows and, in knowing, can do. The guests will be fed. Her hands turn to the work before them with the certainty of skill and long experience. Her eyes observe, and whatever comes as a demand she turns willingly to meet, for there is space now in which to move. "But one thing is needed," and now the possibility exists of meeting that need: to be wholly Martha and wholly Mary, and not just fractions of herself.

It is this struggle that the craftsman faces, perhaps always, whenever work begins. I have seen carpenters work in what I thought was utter chaos: piles of wood shavings, tools scattered with abandon, no drawings or plans—or, if plans were there, they were buried in the shavings. Yet, when the need arose, the hand found the chisel without hesitation, and the shape of the wood conformed itself, as if by magic, to the mind's blueprint. Was there a moment just before work began in which the craftsman took stock of the workbench and of himself? Was there such a moment's pause in which the cares and troubles about many things gracefully took their proper place in the background so that a space could appear in front, so that the eye could see and the ear could hear and the hand could grasp with assurance the tool and material, and work could begin?

The turning of the attention to any new endeavor implies a change of direction and a moment in which that change could take place. One may liken the process, perhaps, to the trajectory of a ball thrown in the air: there comes a moment when the upward and outward direction changes and the return to earth begins. The masters of the Japanese Tea Ceremony, who drew on much of the experience of craftsmen in shaping the ceremony itself, gave a place of honor to just such a moment, called by them "the moment of no-choice": that moment when, the utensils of tea having been assembled in their proper places, the host pauses for an instant, takes stock of himself, and knows that, in the words of Rikyu, there is only one need: "to boil water, make tea, and serve it." There is no choice to be made, no "should I do this or that," but simply the following of the direction already chosen, the continuation of the process.

For this to take place, the craftsman needs knowledge, skill, craft—as well as his tools and materials. The need for things to

be made—blankets, pots, or cabinets—can be seen in an inner
as well as an outer sense. The outer sense—my need (or
yours) for a blanket in which to keep warm, for a pot from
which to eat, for a cabinet to hold the blanket or pot—is plain.
But the craftsman must be in touch with another need: his need
to work, his need to exercise the knowledge which he has spent
his apprenticeship in getting, his need to follow with the attention not only the outward shaping of the thing but also the inward shaping of himself. For this he must have free time and
space, in both the inner and outer senses. He must have a
workshop and the time to work in it; he must have an inner
freedom from the troubles and concerns of the rest of his life,
time and space within so that the attention has room in which
to follow the movements of the hands.

Well, my infidel self observes, even when on very rare occa-
sions such a state of mind and heart and body is reached, it
does not last very long. Soon I am back in my old rut, worrying
and resenting and rattling the mental dishes as usual. Suddenly
the wood shavings swallow up all my tools, the movement of
the wheel falters, and the centered clay goes awry; the shuttle
of red thread, which was in hand just a moment ago, has
vanished entirely.

At such moments, there are several possibilities. I can stop
what I am doing, perhaps to begin again from the beginning.
Or I can continue, try to find the thread again, center the clay
again, take stock for a moment and try to find the space and
time to work here and now. Not an easy thing: as hard—
perhaps harder—than finding that state the first time. But now
it may be that something is possible again because it has happened once before. Unfortunately, there is no formula and I
must again find the possibility by searching for it. It may entail
some suffering: suffering one's own emptiness, dryness, seeing
its manifestation in the material results of my work.

It is necessary to begin again and again—to repeat the movement, but not for the sake of making it habitual, for that would be to betray the teaching of the craft. Rather, the repetition is necessary in order to know, in order to bring my fragmented and fugitive parts together under the set of laws that governs all craft and find the freedom in those laws. My inner nature will not suffer extinction by such obedience, except when I fall into the habitual. I need attention, in order to know my inner nature and to protect myself from the habitual, or just to observe when habit appears. In such a moment of real choice, I can find the free time and space in which to begin again.

Perhaps this is the meaning and purpose of apprenticeship. It has been said that the apprentice is the one who tries to remember the countless things that his master has taught him; the master is he who knows only the one thing: his craft.

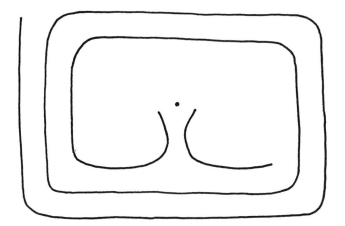

"*I become oblivious of any reward to be gained or any fame to be acquired. When I am free from the influences of all such outer considerations, I can listen to the inner voice which tells me clearly what I have to do.*"

III: *A BRASS ANGEL*

In Ezekiel 40–43, the prophet is transported to the top of a very high mountain overlooking "the frame of a city on the south"—the site of what is to be the New Temple. His guide on this adventure is an angel "whose appearance [is] like the appearance of brass, with a line of flax in his hand, and a measuring reed," and the brass angel proceeds to reveal to Ezekiel what one commentator has called "visionary blueprints of the reconstructed Temple and the New Order in the Holy Land."[1] The peroration is worth quoting in full.

Thou son of man, shew the house to the house of Israel, that they may be ashamed of their iniquities: and let them measure the pattern.

And if they be ashamed of all that they have done, shew them the form of the house, and the fashion thereof, and the goings out thereof, and the comings in thereof, and all the forms thereof, and all the ordinances thereof, and all the forms thereof, and all the laws thereof: and write it in their sight, that they may keep the whole form thereof, and all the ordinances thereof, and do them.

This is the law of the house; upon the top of the mountain the whole limit thereof round about shall be most holy. Behold, this is the law of the house.

Authority rings clear, even to the iniquitous, even in translation; unaccommodating and strict, this is an angel speaking. He first annunciates the idea of a sacred structure ("the house"), then the particular "forms" it will take (its shape and function in space and time), and finally the "law" governing its conception, execution, and use: it is a holy work.

At first it would seem as though this idea were imposed upon the worker from on high as corrective punishment for ill-doing; indeed, not only the old stories but also much firsthand experience say that work in our fallen world is essentially penal. At any rate it *is* an angel speaking and what can a worker do but (ashamed or not) conform, "measure the pattern," and continue in that measure until the work is done?

And yet Ezekiel observes that the brass angel manifests himself in a curiously workmanlike guise . . . an uncommon sort of foreman perhaps. Whatever their symbolic function, the flaxen line and measuring reed are also instruments for use on the job, while brass itself seems pointedly unremote and exoteric—serviceable and tough, in fact. And the idea the angel brings with him has an energy to it that—according to Ezekiel's transcription—touches what might be thought of as the worker's conscience. It may be wise to hear the brass angel as an inner authority rather than one imposed from on high. Or perhaps, since an angel is by definition an intermediary, there is less of a quarrel than is commonly assumed between "above" and "below."

"Shew the house," he demands, "that they may be ashamed." But "the house," the Temple, no longer exists at this point in its material aspect. It is, then, the *idea* of the Temple, now to be reactivated by means of the prophet Ezekiel, that can touch the shattering emotion called "shame" and initiate the process of self-rectification and renewal. For shame has a positive function; it cannot be imposed and yet without it the idea will fall on dull ears or appeal to the mind alone. Shame is an intimate emotional event, an opening, the affective recognition of a personal responsibility: there is a higher authority that my life has lost touch with and I must set about seeking it. Seek and ye shall find, but first one must know one is lost. So the pilgrim Dante has first of all to "refind" himself (*mi ritrovai* are the poet Dante's exact words) astray in a dark wood and feel the shame of his life before he is able to perceive his spiritual guide, who perhaps has been there all the time. So, in the epiphany of the brass angel, word of the house troubles and awakens conscience. The shock of shame revives an authority hidden within.

"And if they be ashamed," the angel continues, "shew them the form of the house." It is only in a state of wakened conscience that the worker is able to measure the pattern of the work at hand; only then can he take the proper steps, can he *make his way,* toward its actualization. In the sense that in realizing his work he realizes himself, the worker is no longer distinguishable from his work. And the brass angel calls such work sacred: "upon the top of the mountain the whole limit thereof round about shall be most holy. Behold, this is the law of the house."

Ezekiel's vision is much more than a vision of the reconstructed Temple of the future. In fact, it is about *now,* about beginning to work, about how this beginning must arise out of a free act of intention on the part of the worker. Poised to start, he is attentive to a high idea and he affirms its authority within him.

How far such a vision of work is from, say, Karl Marx's vision of it as an "alienation of life"! It is no dismissal of Marx's acute and troubling diagnosis of contemporary labor conditions to say that he was not dealing with an *idea* of work at all, at least as we are seeking to develop it in these pages. The dictionary defines labor as a passive action, a being-acted-upon, a travail or toil etymologically related to the Latin *labare,* "to slip or lapse" (most probably referring to the imposed burden underneath which one staggers). In contrast to the brass angel's worker, a laborer is not agent but patient. (So convicts are sentenced to hard labor, never hard work.) What Simone Weil experienced in the Renault plant was in effect her *work* becoming *labor,* her initiative of self-dedication and affirmation turning automatic, alien, oppressive "in the circuit of inert matter."

For now, perhaps the most helpful historical analogue to the idea of the worker as envisaged by the brass angel is the idea of apprenticeship developed in the various guild systems and surviving still in certain craft or workers' organizations—the French Compagnons du Devoir, to take one current example.*

The apprentice is he who knows he needs a master, who seeks until he finds him, who—having found him—studies and works to make a master in or of himself. Apprenticeship, then, means a relationship with a higher authority, freely undertaken by the lesser. Thus I may wish to apprentice myself to a certain master builder in Oslo or to a master potter in Cornwall. In such cases, the authority is felt to be "external" (I go, as a seeker, to someone else) and so in a sense it is. On the other hand, it is I who wish to enter upon this relationship; the initiating act, the acknowledgment of need and undertaking of proper direction, comes from me. And this, too, within me, has to do with higher authority.

The Compagnons call this sort of action, this work, *le devoir,* duty. But duty to what? one may ask; or to whom? The answer offered by the brass angel is: to oneself. To the authority, to the master, who is resident within.

* *"Compagnonnage* is a workers' organization whose end is the professional, moral, and spiritual perfection of its members."[2] French archives furnish public records of its existence from the fourteenth century on, but what one grasps of its iconography and rites suggests a much older, esoteric past. In general, its emblems relate to the linked themes of "sacred building" and "master builder," in particular to the raising of the Temple in Jerusalem. Information is available from the organization's Paris headquarters.

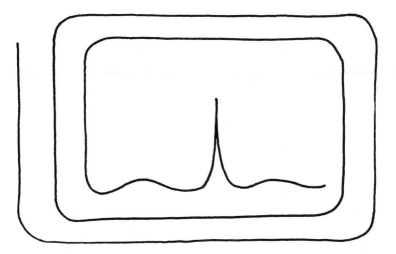

"When my skill is thus concentrated, I take up my ax; I make sure that it is perfectly sharp, that it fits my hand and swings with my arm. Then I enter the forest."

IV: *THE HAND AND THE TOOL*

A job needs doing. I am in front of it. (Or, just as likely, I am in it before I know it.) I may pause to ponder the image of a brass angel, the notion of service to a higher authority. It is an appealing prospect—that my workaday task might be transformed, even if only momentarily, into something extraordinary. But philosophical considerations aside, the job *still* needs doing. I have to get down from brass angels to brass tacks.

I am here, looking for what might be here. Maybe there's an angel here, maybe not; it's not my business. I think about what needs to be done. Perhaps it's as simple a thing as fixing a cold frame for my wife's garden; or a big project like making a new patio out of block and stone; or maybe something more abstract, like writing this chapter. The job could well be the sort of thing we are pleased to call "craft," or "art," but for the moment we will not draw any such distinctions. I visualize how I will do it, maybe I draw a plan, I try to see the whole and the parts, I gather my materials and my tools, and I set to work I try to move cleanly, to be orderly, careful, to have my wits about me. I conceive each step of the work "defensively" (I take Murphy's Law seriously). That's my ordinary way, and it's not a bad place to start. I need my ordinary habits and approaches. They will get the job done.

But they will not summon an angel. More is required—or perhaps less: "One thing is needed." As I work, I try to stay a little free, to watch, listen, feel. The work goes on and I am with it, but I also try to explore within that. I try to stay active, immediate, practical. I search for my relationship to the work, to matter, to the tool, to the hand, to myself, in this moment and no other. Still no angel? Patience. In the present instance, I focus on the pen that is actually in my hand. For, as I write, I can begin to explore what is taking place. Curious black marks are coming out of the pen. It is moving rapidly, faster than the mind can follow, yet it fails to keep pace with the mind's movement. My thought bounces around, now coming out through the pen onto the paper, now evaporating, now lingering to reconsider what has already emerged, now rearranging things, resculpting, repolishing—and again and again searching out what is actually happening.

I look for the connection between the pen and the thought. I suspect that there must be a hand in here somewhere, and I locate it for a moment, from the inside, an intricate network of muscles, nerves, bones, dancing somewhere between the thought and the pen. The muscles seem unnecessarily tight and willful; I notice that behind them is a straining forearm, a knotted stomach, a tense jaw, neck, forehead. Once observed, the tensions fall back a little, and for a moment the pen glides a bit more freely, linked not to a hand in isolation but to the organic sensation of a whole body. Indeed, the pen almost seems to connect with watchfulness itself, with a continuous current of life that, I am suddenly aware, is pouring into me. In such a moment, words that surprise even the writer may appear on the paper.

And then, instantly and imperceptibly, the connection is broken; the thought loses touch with the experience; and the words, though they keep coming, cease to be informed with life; they become deformed, passing as they must through all manner of unseen bottlenecks before emerging chaotically onto the page. This is a crucial moment. I have touched something, and now it is gone. I doubt, perhaps lose interest, or make excuses. Indeed, doubts such as these, variously formulated and variously suffered, will come again and again, and—unless one simply throws up one's hands—they can act as a force of germination and growth.

I take a fresh look at my hand and am perhaps astonished this time at the very sight of it. It is an awesome thing—mine and not mine. Among other things, I notice that its structure is uncommitted; it is not frozen into a specialized form such as a hoof or a paw but is free enough—as well as sensitive and intelligent enough—to take up any number of tools and perform highly varied and exacting tasks. A marvelous entity, its very existence calls for the master craftsman to appear, to occupy it, and to give it direction. It is from the emptiness of this hand that all tools, all crafts, all human creations come into being. And it is through the emptiness of this hand that a miracle could pass to leave its imprint on matter.

I look at the pen in my hand. I imagine for the moment that it is just a stick. If I grasp the stick by holding my thumb on the same side as my fingers, the ways I can manipulate it are limited. Once I bring my thumb around the stick to oppose my fingers, it is transformed. Before, it could only crudely push, perhaps dig or prod. Now, with my thumb pressing against it, able to shift it with more exactitude—to clench it so it carries the full force of the arm, even the body, along its length or to hold it lightly against the fingertips, like a needle—the stick becomes a precision tool. With it, one can shape things, bring about a finer control over the hand's activity. Not only has the stick more potential energy through being in my hand, but I see also that my own energy can be conserved by the way I use it. The stick has many possibilities. Shape it this way or that, use different materials, and it becomes an ever-growing variety of tools, applications of myself. With a serrated edge, the stick becomes a saw; with a honed flat end, a chisel; with a weight fastened to its end, a hammer.

But behind all these tools is a hand, and behind the hand a man—a man working not merely to fulfill a particular physical need, but working also, and especially, out of the human necessity for creation. If the purpose of a tool is to fulfill a necessity, to bridge a gap, then what kind of a tool is man, and what specific necessity does he or might he fulfill?

Relationship with the tool gives a workman his skill, and a long apprenticeship is needed to master a tool and its interactions with the material. But mastery is not merely something that is reached, nor is quality simply an end to be arrived at; rather, mastery is an opening into an inner world in which a new authority and new qualities can begin to be felt.

So I see that how I use the tool depends on how I use myself. To what are my actions a response? What, if anything, do they obey? There is a kind of listening which puts me into a flow, brings me in touch with the life rhythm of myself. It almost seems that one couldn't say where the tool ends and where "myself" begins. In certain crafts, where tools do not intervene between the hands and the material, the hands themselves are the tools; there is no difference in principle between a bare hand shaping clay and a hand-held hammer shaping iron. The tool, and indeed anything one uses, becomes for the moment an extension of oneself, not figuratively but literally, for the tool functions as a kind of spigot through which one's force is measured and dispensed to the outside world. The same can be said, on a higher level, of the hand, and one may even come to look upon the physical body and all its working parts as yet another order of tool. Pursuing this line finally to the inner world, the world of feeling, thought, subtle sensation, one finds it more difficult to speak in terms of a "tool" because one is less clear about what or who is operating what or whom, but one can envision, in potential at least, a well-ordered inner workshop at the service of something higher still. "Whatsoever thy hand findeth to do, do it with thy might" (Ecclesiastes 9:10). On this level, it would seem that a free attention is the only tool. But with my attention held captive in varying degree by any number of extraneous motifs—my ambition for the work, anxiety, impatience, frustration, an empty stomach—I see that, in short, it is myself who is in the way and who impedes such a connection.

It is at this point, perhaps, that a new question emerges: Is it possible to become invisible, to *be there* only for the sake of seeing what the work needs and to give it that, no more but no less, to help it forward in the direction it wants to go, to *use* the tool, to *use* the hand, truly to *use* myself? Perhaps this is not such a new idea. For here, it would seem, is the rationale behind the traditional craftsman's insistence on anonymity. Surely it did not come from some sentimental notion about humility; more likely it was a simple matter of practicality: he wanted to get out of the way.

Thus, the tool in my hand, insofar as it is the (relatively) known end of a chain whose other end is unknown, becomes two-headed. As one head works on the material in front of me, the other works on me, reminding me that I am in the presence of an unanswered question. Here is a tool, a point of contact between the outer and the inner world. With my hand, I feel it; with my eyes, I see work emerging beneath it. Clearly something is having an impact on the world; it is that something that is in question.

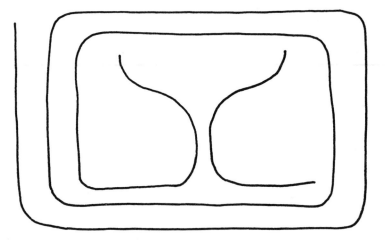

"I look for the right tree: the tree that is waiting to become my table. And when I find it, I ask: 'What have I for you, and what have you for me?'"

V: *THE APPRENTICE*

In the field, tended by man, the seed grows to maturity, endur-
ing darkness and light, moisture and heat. These natural forces
shape and transform the embryonic plant, nurturing it and
bringing it to its culmination before the harvest. After the
harvest, a new life begins, the grain or grape is crushed, mixed
with other substances, allowed to ferment under the watchful
eyes of vintner or baker, and brought to another culmination as
bread or wine. The craftsman takes material in its natural state
and gives to it the possibility of becoming something of a
different level—a vehicle for the expression of laws of a higher
order of nature, a doorway between the sacred and profane, a
channel of power for the reciprocal flow of human and divine
energies. This is what the craftsman gives his material, but it is
also this which the material gives the craftsman: his own possibility of becoming such a vehicle, such a doorway, such a channel.

The craftsman does not begin his life as a master. There
must be a certain knowledge, gained in apprenticeship, upon
which the craft may itself be shaped. "We received all the
members of our body at the first Creation, after all other things
had been made," the alchemist-philosopher Paracelsus wrote in
the fifteenth century:

But the knowledge that man needs was not yet in Adam but was given him only when he was expelled from Paradise. . . . What man can give an account of or explain how he learned to till the soil, to raise vines, or to make cheese? No one, unless he can point to his teacher, and so on and so on, until we come to the first teacher. And to whom can he point? To no one except to Him who created man; for He also gave him Knowledge . . . At the first creation there was everything, but not "art" nor the light of nature. But when Adam was driven out of Paradise, God created the light of nature for him by ordering him to gain subsistence through the toil of his hands . . . only then did "the inner man," "the man of the second creation," come into being.[1]

What is the process of learning, of apprenticeship? There are many theories but they come to this: we learn by observation, by imitation, and by that fortuitous kind of thinking which discerns the connection between two observations and links them into an idea. Under the craftsman's eye, the wood yields to the chisel, the iron spreads under the hammer, the clay takes shape from the cupped hands. The apprentice's imitative movements give form to the materials under the hand and tool, and at the same time the nature of the materials—the resistance, texture, and tendencies of clay, wool, iron, or wood—inform him not only about themselves, but about himself as well. The hand manipulates, and the observing eye and ear receive confirmation or denial of the experiment. At times, by the grace of a momentary receptivity, a connection is made between inner and outer movements, and a new knowledge is gained.

We begin with observation. But how to observe? The untutored eye and ear observe too much and too little, for in the beginning, the apprentice does not know what is important and what is not. What he needs to acquire is a working knowledge of the materials under the hands. But observation is difficult: one is easily distracted, the attention led astray by a momentary fancy. What is needed is an attention free enough to follow movements of increasing complexity, disciplined enough not to be caught by a fleeting interest. Distraction is but one obstacle to observation. Others— boredom, ambition, envy, impatience—all conspire to lead me into despair. The question arises, whether apprenticeship does not have as much to do with acquiring mastery over the internal circumstances as over the external characteristics of tools and materials. There is a Japanese story of a master swordsman who put his apprentice into the scullery. Each day, as the lad was washing dishes, the master would creep up behind him and give him a tremendous whack across the shoulders with a stick. Before long, the apprentice had learned not only to expect the blow, but to avoid and even parry it. Such was his first lesson in swordsmanship.

Ultimately, the master hands over a tool to his apprentice, and a new stage of learning begins. Now, relying on his continuing observation of the master, trying to imitate the movements, and comparing the results with the model before him, the apprentice brings his body into the same discipline as his feelings. In attempting to imitate his teacher, the apprentice sees at once when his actions fail to be as precise as the master's. As time goes on, the apprentice acquires an expertise, and the results of his work more and more resemble that of his teacher. On his own, he is forced to fall back on a memory of the prototype: to do it this way or that? To the extent that he recognizes his inability to achieve the given form, he realizes that he is still far from a mastery of the craft. He returns to his former place as pupil: to watch and to relearn what was forgotten.

One obstacle to imitation, in the sense of trying to follow a model, is habit. How can actions be creative if only old habits are in control? One walks this way, sits this way, puts hands to the tools and materials the same way again and again, out of force of habit. There is no freshness, no new life out of which could come the energy of creation, and work is done with less precision, care, and interest.

It might be said that the path of apprenticeship merely leads from one set of habits to another, that I replace a set of interests by an obsession. What craft can there be in learning by rote another person's way of working? Is there no place for freedom of expression in craft? When the apprentice becomes simply a clever imitator of his master, surely there is no craft. A machine could do as well: no, a machine could do better, for the machine, if it is well made and well suited to its task, will "obey the rules" unerringly and will achieve a mathematically precise symmetry that is perhaps unattainable by even the greatest masters. There are now computers which can even learn from "mistakes" and correct their "behavior." But a computer cannot learn to *make* a mistake, to risk failure for the sake of discovering something new. It cannot perform the intuitive type of thinking which links, however loosely at first, two apparently disparate observations and finds in that linking a new idea, a new expression of a law. So for the apprentice who does not make that self-initiatory leap, habits of thought and movement dictate forever the results of his craft, whether they are old, untutored habits or newly acquired imitations of someone else's. Yet without observation and imitation, the discipline of attention needed to make such a leap cannot come into being.

To examine the process of learning a craft, I undertook to study the Japanese Tea Ceremony and for a while apprenticed myself to a master of the Urasenke school, which has a branch in New York City. My apprenticeship was undoubtedly not long enough for me either to become a master or even perhaps to learn to the fullest the experience of apprenticeship, so what I relate in the following pages must be taken for what it is: an early encounter with some of the inner difficulties, and perhaps also the possibilities, in craft work.

From the beginning, my teacher encouraged me to bring a guest to participate in the Tea Ceremony, a circumstance which at first puzzled me because I knew that my movements were clumsy and that I needed constant guidance. I was to see later the value of this condition, even when, as I thought, my movements were more graceful and I no longer needed to be told what to do next. It is perhaps only when the movements have become more or less "known" and familiar that the real problems could be encountered. Until that time, learning was purely an outer experience—or would have been if, from the first, guests had not watched every move.

As I moved through my instruction, week by week, the careless and habitual ways of moving became less and less powerful, as the intention toward a graceful and effortless—that is, tensionless—cycle of gestures and postures took over. If only a single lesson was skipped, the old habits immediately took control again, and my western foot came down boot-hard on the *tatami* mats as I crossed the tea room. Again and again my instructor would have me enter the room until I crossed it, if not as gracefully as possible, at least more quietly. "In carrying utensils," he would tell me, patiently repeating the litany of my apprenticeship, "what is heavy must seem light, what is light, heavy. Only thus are all things handled with equal care. Remember that nothing in this room has any more importance than anything else, not even yourself."

I try to remember this as I set down the bowl of water and go out to bring in other utensils, only to forget the instant I leave the room and my instructor's impassive and watchful gaze. One or two at a time, I bring the tea things into the room, turning to close the door again only when the last items—the

waste-water receptacle, together with the bamboo water dipper
and its stand—are in hand. I start to turn toward the room but
Yamada-san's quiet voice stops me in my tracks.
"Ah! No, start again." I begin to burn with embarrassment. I
start to turn.
"Ah! No, again." Now I am on fire, my hand trembles a little
and the dipper clatters to the floor. As gracefully as I can—
considering that I am now less than eighteen inches from the
closed door—I kneel and retrieve the dipper. I replace it in its
delicate balance across the top of the waste-water receptacle. I
shift my left foot back and begin to turn.
"Start again."
Then a deep silence grows inside me. There is, for just a moment, no thought of my guest or my foolishness. There is no
question about what to do then, and my right foot crosses over
my left at the toe and I turn with ease, cross the mats, and take
my place. The moment of silence passes almost the instant I
move and I glance at Yamada-san's face for a hint of praise for
being right. Not a trace of praise is there; that round moon of a
face is not even looking at me, but has turned to explain something to my guest.
I take my place and adjust my trouser knees so they are not
so tight. Now there is time again, and, as if from a distance, I
hear Yamada-san explain to my friend that this is the moment
called "no-choice"; there is nothing to do except follow Rikyu's
precept: boil water, make tea.
In that moment, there is a renewal. I pull the purple silk nap-
kin (*fukusa*) from my belt—
"Ah!"
No? I replace the *fukusa* and move the waste-water receptacle. I pick up the dipper, allow it to pivot under my fingers until
it is upright before me. I am looking now into the cup of the
dipper, and I hear Yamada-san explaining:

"This is called the 'mirror position.' It allows the host, in examining the dipper, to see something else, as if he were looking in a mirror. . . ." I find my intention again—to serve tea—in the second before I continue with my preparations. Then I again begin to move.

At last I can take out the *fukusa* and clean the utensils with it. My anticipation of pleasure rises because the folding of this square piece of silk appears intricate to the uninitiated, and I forget that its simplicity is deceptive. Embarrassment replaces pleasure—not because my guest will have seen my clumsiness, but because Yamada-san has.

"Try again." I look up at my guest, but there is no judgment on her face: this is all new to her, fresh. I refold the *fukusa*, taking time and care. I continue.

Step by step, the ceremony unfolds. The time comes to put the powdered green tea into the tea bowl. I reach for the spoon.

"Ah! Not yet."

I stop, completely at a loss as to how I will continue. The dipper? No. The waste-water jar? No. The tea bowl? No. Surely I am right; it is the spoon that is next. I reach for the spoon.

"No!"

No? Then what? I try frantically to remember, and each second burns like fire. My clumsiness is now surely obvious, but my friend is looking down, either sharing my embarrassment or trying not to further excite my confusion. Thoughts race around my head and I feel like getting up and leaving. I try to rehearse what has gone before, remembering each step in the process, but this only adds to the turmoil. I look at Yamada-san, hoping that he will hint at or betray the next step.

"I can't remember," I say, my throat dry as bone. Yamada-san sits and waits, his face impassive. He opens his fan and shuts it, perfectly at ease, content to wait as long as it takes.

This is the lesson. Something in me relaxes. I still do not remember, but now there is no panic. I wait. I know, and the knowledge will come. I will remember, in time.

And of course I do; and then, quietly, the rest of the ceremony flows into place. The tea is made, whisked to a froth, the bowl turned so that the mark on its side faces the guest. As she drinks from it, I sit quietly, no longer rehearsing. There was no blinding flash of revelation; there was a moment in which I could not remember the form, the right movement, the proper order of things, and in the next moment, the knowledge was in my hands, renewed. Will the renewal last forever? Or will I again forget the form and be in need of another impulse to maintain the momentum of my intention? As for the possibility of creativity in such a formalized setting, now is not the time to raise such a question, seeing that I have not even mastered the rudiments of the craft. What creativity can come when I am still fettered by habit and inattention? If the place for creative harmony between the elements of the Tea Room is in relation to the guest, must I not be free enough to see the guest and not just myself, in order to choose the right bowl, the right flowers, the proper scroll? One is aiming at the simplicity of Rikyu's formula. If I am at ease with what I am doing, there will then be the possibility of making my guests feel at ease and to engage in the conversational play that is proper to that setting, which has to do with the establishment of relationships.

A certain Zen master, who was also a master of tea, once had as a guest a Hollywood celebrity. The ceremony began: with great care, the room was made ready, all the utensils were chosen in accordance with the principles of harmony among season, guest, and circumstance, the flowers placed in the bamboo vase demonstrated the rules of tea-room flower arrangement. Each utensil was brought in with care, the door was closed, and host and guest were seated. The ceremony began.

Water was boiled. The master placed the bowl before him. Then, with as much precision and grace as in all the ceremony before, the master took from his sleeve a Lipton tea bag, made tea, and served it.

But then, he was a master.

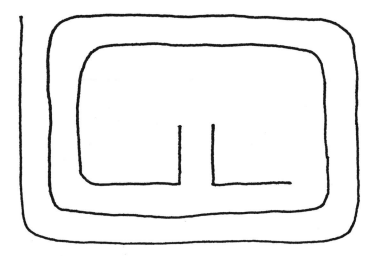

"Then I cut down the tree and set to work."

VI: *CLOSE TO ZERO*

How frequently, and how briefly, does the craftsman touch the material as he builds. Yet these short touchings are the sparks of a fire that forms. During the building of an object, these touchings occur hundreds or thousands of times, repetitively and with small differences. In increments the material is turned into the product of the craft. By means of his fingers or the tools in his hands, the craftsman supplies what is needed for the object as it grows. The material is changed into a form that somewhere has been determined, somewhere planned.

Thus a way reveals itself.

The craftsman's methods, tools, and materials can be thought of as extensions or even aspects of one another. In the most obvious way the material dictates his tools and methods. But from a larger view, out of these three elements of his work, he forms a single tool, an ableness in himself which knows the proper way of working. Such a tool is not formed easily or soon, but it is worked for. Of all possible tools, it is the one most adapted to his needs. It has the thinnest and the broadest edge, the stiffest and most flexible blade, the widest and narrowest surface. It fits every requirement of his craft. With use it retains its properties and even enhances them, but without use they waste away.

The development of such a tool is common among crafts-men, and, at the same time, it is unique to each craftsman. He carries it with him always. It allows him to repeat what he is doing and to work in a way that will develop it further. He finishes his work in the shortest time, yet is rested. The objects that he makes will be satisfying to his customers.

What way of working will permit him to develop such a tool? The answer is simple but its realization is difficult. The answer is his ability to move in a nearly straight line, to work with min-imum distraction, to control to the utmost degree his human strength. His patience must know no veering, he must contain his efforts and work from within. The material of the craft re-sponds properly only when it is guided by so proper a tool.

He senses the movement of his hand until the line of its working is like a nerve in him.

In patience he finds the possibility of all his accomplish-ments. His needs move aside as they arise. At every mo-ment he works close to a boundary, an invisible wall that defines the path to the next moment, that moves ahead of him as he follows it, a wall that he never quite touches. Patience in the craftsman is the willingness to recognize and obey the movement of this wall. At each stroke of the tool he brings his work up to it. His wish is as slight as the separating of the next fibers of wood, the rising of the next particles of clay. His thoughts and movements are bounded by the wall. His emotion makes nearness to the wall satisfying to him. When he has finished the movement, the wall moves beyond, establishing the further step. Again he moves close to it. The movements of the wall and the craftsman are nearly continuous, nearly the same.

He remains aware of this process. He never permits the wall to be beyond the periphery of his inner vision. He attends to the material without losing sight of the wall. This is the highest degree of his patience. If he attempts to ignore the wall, to go beyond it without completing the movement, he will lose the wall. He will be without direction. For him, the wall provides a way; it makes his progress possible. Moment by moment, he follows the wall. Perhaps the wall is the same as the guides that we meet in myths and legends. Can you hear it? It is the sound of the edge moving into the wood, of the mallet descending, of the thin slip of the shuttle, of fingers on clay. It is the small sound heard when the craftsman produces just the motion that is required. He works near to the wall, near to the boundary. The distance is almost zero. At the times when I work like this, I am a craftsman. But such times are rare.

One of the craftsman's satisfactions is to find ways in which his work can be done most quickly. He learns to use his tools well, to work with the smallest number of them, to find their widest applications. In his hands each tool produces a secure framework. He finds pleasure in the tool itself, in its being the product of another craft.

The craftsman works with no pride in accomplishing, but with a joy in accomplishing. His ableness helps him to experience the difference. The utmost in inner relaxation will lead him to the joy. The material moves under his hands. He guides or follows it, hardly knowing which. He works to know the imperceptible difference. Suddenly, joy becomes pride, and he loses the sense of his movement. The transformation is quick and as certain as his image in a mirror. He tries to look beyond his pride by once more not looking in the old way. He calls upon the part of him that rests. As he tries, pride goes; joy comes again. With no other demand he continues in this way. The material he works with is flexible and fluid.

For quite a while, his working is pure. Then he knows it is pure, and the old thoughts come again.

A fullness emanates from the craftsman's way of working that fills his shop. This fullness is present in everything he builds; it is the emotional content of his work. According to the material he works with, it is roundness, or depth, or extension. It is the essence of containing. In all that he undertakes, an equality pervades the dimensions, the directions are secure. The object is bounded by that which alone can complete it. The true extent of his work can never be denied.

The workshop is designed to complement this fullness, both in the beginning and as the shop grows. This property in the shop is a valuable aid to his work. It is achieved through his selection of the tools, his placement of them, the shapes and locations of the benches, by whatever else is needed. In so real a sense can the shop be said to exist around the craftsman. It exists quietly, as a plant grows. As he works, he makes small adjustments in the fullness to correspond to the need of the object he is building. Thus the shop is a little different for everything he builds. Now one part is changed slightly to be a point of rest, another to be a point of tension. Through these changes he reinforces the intent in his work. The quality of what he builds will profit by them.

By the sight of the first bench you see in the shop, you will know the quality of the work being done there. All the parts of the shop partake of this quality, even the dust on the floor.

In the same way the energy in him moves and is balanced.

Much more of the craftsman's strength goes into the use of his tools than ever is needed by the material. Indeed, it is by means of this excess strength that he gains control of the tool. The material resists; the tool overcomes. There is no need here for extra strength. Yet the extra strength is there in the tool— not potentially nor in abeyance, but there. Whether he works with a chisel on wood, a shuttle through threads, or his fingers on clay, the craftsman in part holds back at the same time that he pushes the tool forward. Thus he adds his own resistance to the resistance of the material and then provides the extra strength needed to overcome it. He resists in the same direction as the material. In general, if the material resists more, he resists more; if the material resists less, he resists less. With so great a proportion of the resistance coming from him, the resistance of the material is relatively small. The material yields in an atmosphere that is always close to zero—the finest control becomes possible.

These opposites—the resistance that he purposefully creates and the strength with which he overcomes it—enable the craftsman to be as if in the material itself. He knows its instant behavior and adjusts to it. His movements may be sudden or slow, or they may be defeated, but there is no surprise. The notice he receives from the material is continuous with its movement. He listens as the wood awakens, as the clay stirs.

The progression of the work as the steps are completed is for him a joy. An energy in him grows from these completions and beginnings. The energy is renewed in the interval between successive steps. It flows into the new direction and moves at the speed of the new step.

He must be able to pivot quickly, to change direction whenever he needs to find energy again. He experiences his energy decreasing as the old impulse dies. A weariness begins. He steps away from the movement, leaving it to its ending. With this effort of abandonment, energy comes. The immediate direction is reborn. The tool cuts; the hands lift the clay once more. Soon this impulse will die. The spirit behind the human frame redirects it. The craftsman's activity remains in the direction of his aim, but not narrowly so. The work progresses by a letting go and a picking up, like the rise and fall of the wind.

At the end of his work, the object is released. In some other location, perhaps that of the user, a seed will grow again.

The craftsman must be both servant and master of strong inner forces. By his attentiveness to his work he is able to summon them. Yet, though they are willing giants, they are easily lost. It is a difficult game. He wishes their strength to be his, and in that moment it is gone. On the verge of finding it, he speaks of it to himself, and it is lost. He attempts to demonstrate it to others and finds that it has disappeared. On such an edge, not veering forward or backward, the craftsman must live and work. Yet the reward for this way of working is great. When he accepts these forces, not claiming their strength for his own, it is his. It is the energy of creation. The gates so carefully tended open to the incredible meadow, to a path which for that moment belongs to him.

From what has been said, it might be supposed that the craftsman rarely fails in his task. On the contrary, he always fails in some degree. Despite his experience, despite the sureness that he sometimes is able to reach and briefly hold, there is within him, as he works, a hesitation, a doubt, a fear. In the object he produces, it appears as a slight roughness at all the edges. This unsureness is necessary for the growth of both him and his craft. He endeavors to pay no attention to it but to remain at the boundary of what he must do. He cannot be certain of the step until the movement is completed, until the step is done. He knows that he cannot know. But he continues with the movement and does not bend to his fear. Thus he is both master and apprentice in his work.

When he fails, the failure leaves its trace in him and a clearer perception. The trace remains for a time in his memory, but he does not search back. It is like an inner object, a weightless burden that reminds.

He continues to have a need for failure. It is the stopping place, the ultimate reluctance of his effort to continue. As he works, his reluctance accumulates, his tenseness grows. He fails —and is able to start again.

To work instead of everything else, to relax away from distractions, to return to himself—these are the craftsman's tasks.

The work goes easily, but only so far; then difficulty comes. One must encourage oneself from the inside. It is exhilarating to work in this way. No tenseness is allowed. Slowly the difficulty withdraws, having no choice. The craftsman's most powerful tool is himself. At some soft pressure, the material begins to become the form that he wishes it to have. He works without certainty of the result. He expects no more from the material than he can expect from himself. Within its limits, it is strong. He tests it, as the wind tests the leaf-laden stem. He approaches the limits within which it is strong. Whatever the scale of his difficulty, he is able to move in a smaller way. He adjusts his movement to be imperceptibly finer than is needed. He begins again. The movement ends. He begins again. There is a seed that allows the craftsman to begin. Perhaps this is the largest secret of all.

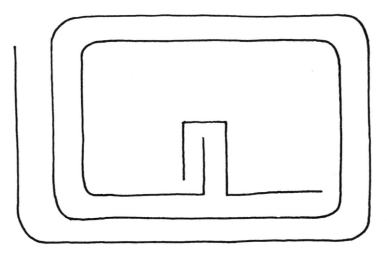

"*I remember how my masters taught me to bring my skill and my thought into relation with the natural qualities of the wood.*"

VII: *WORKING FOR A LIVING*

What has the relative quiet or, at least, the more disciplined movement of the workshop to do with me in my untidy office? I am at my desk early today, with a moment to sit quietly and listen to the question. Is there a craftsmanlike way of working that is available not only to the worker in his workshop, but to the worker wherever he works, whatever his work is—in a factory or bank, in an executive office or houseful of children; even here in a noisy advertising agency?

For a long time these have been academic questions for me, at times interesting me seriously; at other times merely piquing my curiosity, often degenerating into mere doodlings in my mind. Today something is different.

Today I want to know for myself if there is still a way of working that would not only support me physically, but would also support this inner hunger that I feel now: a hunger actually to be here at my job, more awake, instead of dreaming at it, swept along from one minor crisis to the next, from paycheck to paycheck.

The New York drama critic Walter Kerr seems to be speaking my thoughts when, in *The Decline of Pleasure,* he writes: "The work we are doing is more or less the work we meant to do in life [but] it does not yield us the feeling of accom-

plishment we had expected . . . If I were required to put into
a single sentence my own explanation of the state of our hearts,
heads, and nerves, I would do it this way: we are vaguely
wretched because we are leading half-lives, half-heartedly, and
with only one-half of our minds actively engaged in making
contact with the universe about us."[1]

This is part of my concern right now: this half-heartedness,
half-mindedness with which I live my one and only life. It
seems related to the triviality of the work I do, and I would
like to place the blame for my dissatisfaction squarely there. I
begin to dream about a fulfilling work: in a hospital perhaps;
in some use of myself that would satisfy this hunger. Still,
what I am doing is the work at hand. It is my livelihood; it
needs doing. I would wish to find a way to attend to it more
creatively, or at least more carefully, so that it felt more like an
exchange: a giving as well as a taking.

I remember the story of two Zen monks, both prodigious
smokers. Concerned about the question of smoking during their
prayer time, they agreed to consult their superiors. While one
received a stern reprimand from his abbot, the other was given
a pat of encouragement. The unlucky one, greatly puzzled,
asked his friend exactly how he had framed his question. "I
asked," the second monk replied, "whether it was permissible
to pray while smoking."

Maybe this is the kind of care my work needs. To pray while
typing, while answering the phone—would it require a very
different way of praying; a way that Zen monks must come to
through their training—something like that wordless beseeching
one discovers in trying to guide a car along an icy road or in
performing any exacting piece of work under all but impossible
conditions?

I once looked up the origin of the word "prayer" and found
its root is in the Latin precarius—"obtained by entreaty,"
hence implying uncertainty, risk. The plain truth is that in my

usual way of working I feel nothing precarious or risky. Nothing is really at stake. Today, for reasons I don't understand, I feel that something vast and mysterious is at stake, something known only to me, important only to me. I can only call it my being. It's as if my usual way of working serves to sever me from my me-ness, from this new and fragile sense of myself at this typewriter right now.

Before I can go any further with a study of my own work, perhaps I need to ponder the meaning of work in general—in other times as well as in our own—and as I ponder, I sense a kinship between the words "work" and "worship." I begin to suspect that man is physically organized in exactly the way he is, just so that he will need to work in order to live; and it seems possible that the substance required for his own transformation and for the maintenance of the universe is created as a direct result of his work.

"In the sweat of thy face shalt thou eat bread," God told Adam, and if man did not actually *need* to work to feed, shelter, and clothe himself, actually in order to survive, perhaps this essential substance, whatever it is, would never be created. Perhaps, since man was created precisely as he is—exactly this kind of breathing, digesting, thinking, feeling organism—there is a precisely ordered way for him to work and to live in order to serve a universal purpose.

For me this is a fresh thought, this idea that it is man-at-work that serves the universe in a special way; and it sheds new light on the possible meaning of the way of the craftsman. However distracted the cathedral builders must have been, upon occasion, from the spiritual aspect of their work (for surely illness, family problems, all the continuing vagaries of the human condition beset these men as they do us), their inner hunger must have been fed by their way of working, a way indicated by their priests and guild masters who constantly reminded them that they were in the service of something higher, that their work was their means of serving and not an end in itself.

With what heart they must have worked then, entrusting themselves to this higher authority!—this same "heart," perhaps, that set the golden harp (surely a symbol of joy in work) side by side with the tools of gold that were unearthed by archaeologists in the Sumerian city of Ur. The dweller in a golden age or an age of faith seems to have understood that he was living a kind of double life, one in the visible world and one in the invisible. Traditional man was apparently taught from infancy that all that he manifested in his everyday living vibrated invisibly in another dimension and that it was his voluntary attempts to participate in his hidden dimension that set him apart from other living creatures—that made him, in fact, a transformer, a Man.

But today where are such teachers? Where are our priests? Our wise men? I try now to imagine what it would be like to be a member of a guild; to be an apprentice in a workshop at the head of which was a master in the original sense of the word: a man whose craft was truly his own, in his hands and heart and in his bones; a man who could impart the inner as well as the outer element of this craft to those working under him, not just by words and example, but by his very presence.

Guild members, we are told, would begin their day with the master in prayer to the guild's patron saint before turning to the work, and prayers of one kind or another punctuated the whole day. Throughout the day there was the closeness of man to man, the sense of one another's existence, and the exchange between the experienced workers and the novices: the meeting of eyes, the showing and the watching, the speaking and the listening. How different from the usual factories and workplaces of today, where little is "handed" from man to man, where eyes rarely meet, and the human voice cannot always rise above the noise of machinery; where men in their isolation from one an-

other begin to feel a kinship only with their particular machine
—a truck driver with his truck, a printer with his press, even a
copywriter with her typewriter.

There is an instant now in which I feel the limitation of this
kind of kinship, and I wonder how we ever lost touch with one
another and with our sacred heritage. How did we become separated from that other dimension in which our forebears felt
their common humanity and the common authority for their
lives? Our discontent as workers today must stem from this incredible lapse: this mass forgetfulness that we are under any
authority higher than that of our boss, whether he be the factory foreman, the president of the company, or oneself.

Oh, for the ordered structure of the guild workshop! The
strong clear voice of the master "re-minding" me, in the real
sense of that word, to return to the silence. Another completely
fresh thought comes to me now. So many of the rituals of the
traditional societies must have been created for just this call to
inner silence. The beating of drums, the tolling of the Angelus,
the sounding of the ram's horn, the repetition of the sacred syl-
lables in whatever language, the ceremonial dances—all these
mysterious activities that until this moment have appeared to
me like so many quaint customs must have been designed for
just this reminding. And at this moment I am shocked to discover the life going on inside me: the breath coming and going;
the amazing heartbeat. I am here; the thought is here; and a
kind of feeling. I am here in this very ordinary place with a
minute, mundane advertisement to write, but it is my work and
it requires me.

What I constantly forget is that I always have my place. It is
here exactly where I am. Where else could it be? Here is this
life that is uniquely mine, one whole unit of creation that is entirely my place and my responsibility.

I feel a great desire not to lose touch with this feeling-
thought that is with me this morning. I have felt it before: a

wishing for something more for myself or from myself. Is there a master in me to whom I can turn, if—like people in fairy tales—I can wish hard enough? I don't know, but something I have read comes alive for me now: "Wood and stone will teach me what cannot be heard from the master's teaching."

I have no wood or stone, but I have my job; that is my reality for now. "To take what there is and use it," Henry James wrote many years ago, "without waiting forever in vain for the preconceived—to dig deep into the actual and get something out of *that*—this doubtless is the right way to live."[2] A thought from Father Robert Capon's writing stirs vigorously in me. "Adam," he wrote, and he was speaking of twentieth-century Adam, of the likes of you and me, "is the priest of Creation. His truest work is to offer up reality itself, not just a headful of abstractions about it."[3]

It seems as if it could be right here, even in this super-automated, super-franchised, polluted, synthetic age, that I might begin my apprenticeship; right here, now, in this attitude of seeing what is. Perhaps this is the elusive way of working that makes all the difference between the craftsman and the slave— just this reordering of my energies because I want to work this way, because I need to, because I must. The authority is still there. We are not forgotten in spite of our forgetfulness, for natural laws, unlike the ordinances of temporal authority, are never changing. It is the very constancy of these laws that offers us a challenge and a hope. It leaves something up to me; it is for me to seek a way to reconnect with these laws. It is even an obligation, if Simone Weil was right in saying that it is the work of our age to create a civilization "founded upon the spiritual nature of work."[4]

Perhaps it would be just in a daily lifelong attitude of "seeing" that the noisy, chaotic activity I call my job could become a support for my attention instead of a distraction. Perhaps, if I attend to the reality that is in front of me moment by moment

—phone, machine, pencil, boss, coffee—constantly failing, accepting to fail and to begin again—this perfectly ordinary work I do might become extraordinary work, might even become my craft.

The phone is ringing now. The first of my co-workers has arrived and is answering it. The question I began with remains:

Is there a way of working that would support this need I feel actually *to be* here at my work?

The answer, I am sure, is not to be found in my head or in any book, but quite simply in an ever-deepening of the question itself.

I confront the outline I left on my desk last Friday, and I get to work.

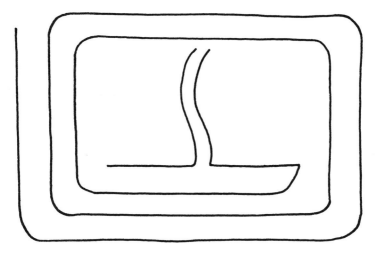

The King said, "When the table is finished, it has a magical effect upon me; I cannot treat it as I would any other table."

VIII: *THE TOUCHSTONE*

In the fifteenth century, Isaac b. Moses ha-Levi wrote:

> Study should always be in beautiful and pleasant books, contain-
> ing harmonious script, written on fine vellum, with luxurious
> bindings, and in pleasant buildings . . . since the beholding and
> study of beautiful forms pleases the soul, urges and strengthens
> its powers.

"Pleases the soul"? We in the twentieth century would not
say it that way, and yet there is a calling echo which responds
to this old-fashioned formulation. A need exists for beautiful
forms that are in harmony with the sacred.

Man has two natures, it is often said; the nature belonging
to the world of Reality, the world of real forms, is asleep; it
has to be "strengthened," it needs to be "pleased" to awake to
itself.

My eye was attracted by a design on a box in an antique
shop window. You haven't time, I told myself, but I was drawn
into the shop. It was a rectangular, wooden cigarette box, well
constructed, with a hinged lid and an arrangement of geomet-
rical patterns inlaid into its top and sides. The patterns were
carefully subdivided so that every element, as in a kaleido-

scope, flowed into the next and began and ended neatly. Clearly, the craftsman who fashioned it was concerned with more than a beautiful box; behind his design one sensed a metaphysical concept.

"It's Japanese," said the store owner. "Nineteenth century." I didn't care when it was made. Harmony, rhythm, proportion, ideas were in it. I had to have the box.

What was the model for the Japanese craftsman? Where did he get his shapes? One senses an order, related to a meaning and source, and the effect on me, at moments, can be one of integration. Whether I know it or not, I am searching for signs of this order wherever I go.

At the time of the building of the mysterious Gothic cathedrals, stonecutters and masons carved messages into the cathedral floors. Eight hundred years later, I walk along the outer circle of the labyrinth at Chartres, and I am reminded—as must have been the intention—of a journey to be made: to another order of being at the Center. Ariadne's thread, my attention, is frail, and I forget, but the impression of a moment of recognition remains.

To evoke this moment is perhaps the only real sense and purpose of art. Real art is a reminder; it relates a thing to an order higher than itself, indicates its place, its nearness or distance from the Center which is also the Self. Traditional artists and craftsmen apply this Pythagorean conception of art, based on geometry and conceived according to a pre-existing system of proportions, to the domain of form.

"We live here among the shadow of things," said the King who was a priest in Robert Louis Stevenson's fable "The Touchstone." The priest-King tests his daughter's suitors by sending them in search of the touchstone. "For in the light of that stone the seeming goes, and the being shows, and all things besides are worthless."

What is the criterion for knowing the quality of a thing in the domain of form? A beautiful form, "well and truly made," is never an end in itself; it is the vehicle, the outward reminder, of a changeless principle behind it. To recognize the quality and the principles which inform it and give it life requires a corresponding quality in oneself, a place that "knows," a touchstone instantly referred to, so that everything can be measured and understood in relationship to it.

"And God said, Let there be lights in the firmament of the heaven to divide the day from the night; and let them be for signs. . . ." Perhaps the whole visible universe can be understood as a symbol, a reminder of the light behind the shadow of things. When symbols are linked in one's mind to the order behind them, they are understood in a different way. An object viewed only on the level of itself will have no objective meaning, but when it is seen as a sign of invisible things, it serves as a support and reminder of another level of being.

I was once the witness to a symbol's transforming power.

There is an old Jewish custom, observed for two thousand years, that on the Ninth of Av, Tisha B'Av, which usually falls in the month of August, Jews pray at the "Wailing Wall," in the Old City of Jerusalem, the Holy City for which the Jewish people have always yearned even when they are there. The Wall is the remnant of the western side of the protecting wall of heavy coursed stones that was built by Herod the Great around the Second Temple. The First Temple, which God commanded King Solomon to build according to a "pattern" revealed to David, was destroyed by the Assyrian armies of Nebuchadnezzar on the Ninth of Av, 587 B.C. The Second Temple, modeled after the pattern of the first and built on the same foundation when the Jews returned from exile in Babylonia, was destroyed by the Romans, also on the Ninth of Av, in A.D. 70.

The Jews lost the Western Wall in 1948, after the United Nations' partition of Jerusalem left it in the Arab land of Jordan. "How is she become as a widow!" Jews mourned on Tisha B'Av. In 1962 I happened to be in Arab Jerusalem on the Ninth of Av, and I went to the Western Wall in commemoration of this day. Israel was still cut off from the site of the Temple then, and when I reached the Wall, below the crest of Mount Moriah, through the Jerusalem labyrinth, there was no one else there.

I stood in front of the deserted stones, guardians of the Temple in which God's presence "dwelled," and said the prayer of Tisha B'Av from the Book of Lamentations: "Turn us to Thyself, O Lord, that we may be turned." It was strange to hear my voice in that empty, silent place. In some mysterious way, the Wall was acting on me. I became aware of the echoes of those who had stood there like this before me. Reminded of them, reminded of the exile to which I then felt linked, another wall, inside myself, seemed to disappear.

Between two heavy ashlars was a small loose stone. I asked forgiveness of the Wall and took it. Some time later, I presented the stone, symbol of the foundation stone of the Temple, on which, according to the Talmud, the whole world rests, to the Hasidic master Abraham Heschel in New York. He utterly ignored it.

"It's from the Western Wall," I told him. Heschel stood up. A tremendous force came into his eyes. He started to touch the now transfigured stone, but reached instead for a *yarmulke* and put it on his head. "This is an event!" he said. He put his hand on the stone and said a Hebrew blessing, the *shehecheyanu,* which gives thanks to God for "letting us reach this moment." Then he sat down. We sat in silence. We were in his office at the Jewish Theological Seminary in the late afternoon, in that moment of questioning light when another order of existence seems to vibrate between two worlds. The figure of Heschel became as still and impersonal as Being. It was as if the Temple was still standing and he had entered it.

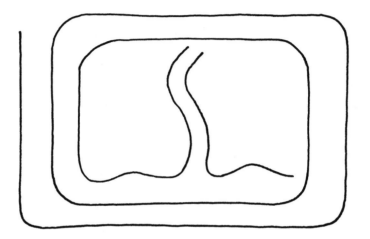

"What is the nature of this magic?"

IX: *MAKE ME A SANCTUARY*

On top of Mount Peor, looking down toward Jeshimon, stood the prophet Balaam. Balak, King of the Moabites, had called on him to curse the Hebrew people who, wandering in the wilderness on their way from Egypt to the Promised Land, seemed to threaten Balak's kingdom. Balaam had accepted the task with one crucial reservation: "The word that God putteth in my mouth, that shall I speak." He would utter only that which was agreeable to the Divine Will.

From the summit of Peor, Balaam saw a sweeping prospect: "all Israel abiding in his tents according to their tribes." He saw a pattern in the wilderness, complex, precise, and shining; to the prophet's eye, a sign and a portent.

Clusters of tents formed a design around a central rectangular court, which was unroofed and enclosed by white curtains of finely woven mesh fabric, hanging on brass pillars with silver capitals. The design conveyed a special meaning: precise and symmetrical, the pillars evenly spaced, the eastern gateway perfectly placed facing the rising sun. Even from such a distance the gate-veil, hung on four copper pillars, shone with beauty, woven of multicolored materials interlaced delicately with gold.

Within the court was an altar approached by a ramp. Four men in priestly robes moved about it. A copper basin near the altar reflected intense light, as if inlaid with thousands of mirrors. Beyond the altar in the courtyard stood a rectangular tent, topped with strips of badger skins which revealed several layers of coverings below. A screen similar to the gate tapestry hung at the entrance on pillars of which only two were discernible, very bright, apparently of gold; and it seemed to Balaam that a fiery cloud was hovering over this point, the center of the pattern.

Balaam gazed and exclaimed: "How goodly are thy tents, O Jacob, and thy tabernacles, O Israel! As the valleys are they spread forth, as gardens by the river's side . . . Blessed is he that blesseth thee, and cursed is he that curseth thee."

The sight that affected Balaam so radically that against the King's demand he pronounced, instead of a curse, an ardent blessing, was the full view of the ancient sanctuary, standing within its court, in the center of the Hebrews' encampment in the wilderness. What was visible to the beholder was only the order, the "art," of a pattern; yet the force that this emanated convinced him of a greater content and turned his tongue to affirmation. The prototype of the sanctuary was shown to Moses on Mount Sinai:

> And the Lord spake unto Moses, saying, Speak unto the children of Israel, that they bring me an offering: of every man that giveth it willingly with his heart ye shall take my offering. And this is the offering which ye shall take of them; gold, and silver, and brass, and blue, and purple, and scarlet, and fine linen, and goats' hair, and rams' skins dyed red, and badgers' skins, and shittim wood, oil for the light, spices for anointing oil, and for sweet incense, onyx stones, and stones to be set in the ephod, and in the breastplate. And let them make me a sanctuary; that I may dwell among them. According to all that I shew thee, after the pattern of the tabernacle, and the pattern of all the instruments thereof, even so shall ye make it. (Exodus 25:1-9)

A midrashic legend speaks of the great perplexity of Moses at this moment. "Surely," he says, "the Divine Presence fills the heavens and the earth; am I to encompass it within the confines of a tabernacle?" And the Holy One responds with an extraordinary simplicity: "My thoughts are not as your thoughts, but erect for me a structure, twenty boards to the north, twenty boards to the south, and eight boards to the west, and I will descend and confine my presence within their bounds."

How can we understand this simple exactitude? According to Exodus, instructions for the housing of this shrine demanded by God Himself begin with a call for the raw materials; these are to be given freely by each person from what he has acquired through his own work, trial, and suffering. The requisitions are specific and the materials called for are precious: gold and silver and brass, onyx, fur, dyes of all colors, silks, linens, oils, and spices—materials of value, but unworked, with possibilities of serving a higher order, of being transformed into a sacred whole. Moreover, the Israelites brought with them not only a store of worldly goods but an experience of the craft of building; as slaves of the Egyptians they had built two treasure cities, Pithom and Raamses, before their departure for the Promised Land. Such practical skills might be considered another sort of raw material now to be transformed through a freely given commitment to a purpose higher than the self-glory of their former masters. The materials called for, then, range from the animal, vegetable, and mineral to the specifically human, but it is man the maker, the craftsman, who must provide the link between the idea coming from a higher level and the substances of all the worlds. In this sense the craftsman is a joiner.

Another law of craft is shown in the precision and the planning, as the instructions for the execution of the Tabernacle continue in Exodus in minute detail, with meticulous measurements, precise placement for every clasp and loop, pin and

cord, and such explicit particulars as the preparation of the
anointing oil and sweet incense, and the design of the priestly
garments. The discipline of precision requires the craftsman's
continued awareness of, and conformity to, the prototype or
projected original, since the fit and fittingness of particulars is
only determined by reference to their part in the vision of the
whole.

A close working relationship among the various craft groups
is also required. Since so much of the lumber is overlaid with
gold or silver or brass, carpenters must consult with metal-
workers; these in turn beat gold into fine thread at the behest of
weavers at work on veils and screens and tapestries. Such scru-
pulous teamwork is made possible by the high aim held in common by all the craftsmen at the site.

The construction of the sanctuary took place under the direct
supervision of master builders, and it is of interest to inspect
their qualifications as given by the traditional texts. For example, the man chosen to be builder-in-chief was Bezaleel, "the
son of Uri, the son of Hur, of the tribe of Judah." It is for good
reason that the Scripture names Bezaleel's grandfather, for Hur
was killed trying to prevent the impatient mob from worshiping
the golden calf, a false god and product, one might say, of a
spiritual avarice and impatience. Patience is a central quality of
the true craftsman, and Hur's descendants—Bezaleel in the
wilderness and Solomon in Jerusalem—would exemplify this
quality during the construction of tabernacle and temple. The
name "Bezaleel" itself, Hebrew for "in the shadow of God,"
suggests something of the inspiration that guided him, as well
as his knowledge of the lore of the Kabbalah. The Bible tells us
that God filled Bezaleel with his spirit, informing the master
builder "in wisdom, and in understanding, and in knowledge
. . . to devise cunning works, to work in gold, and in silver,
and in brass, and in cutting of stones, to set them, and in carving of timber, to work in all manner of workmanship."

Aholiab was appointed to work at Bezaleel's side as journeyman. The two craftsmen, at opposite poles of the social structure, linked the royal tribe of Judah and the lesser one of Dan. The Zohar represents the two craftsmen as symbolizing the energy of the right and the energy of the left, with Moses uniting and balancing the two.

Bezaleel designed and crafted the Holy Ark, the sevenbranched candelabrum, all the vessels for the Tabernacle, and the priestly vestments, and he and Aholiab together instructed the other craftsmen—every "wise hearted man" who had been stirred to work on the sanctuary—in the subtle arts of applying the skills and goods acquired in slavery to the construction of the dwelling place of the Divine Presence.

The plan of the Tabernacle, as first revealed to Moses and transmitted down the years to Bezaleel and his co-workers, is described in the biblical text in such detail that it would be possible to reconstruct it today. It was an exquisitely constructed, portable shrine, which could be erected or dismantled on short notice to be transported through the desert. When the manifestation of Divine Intent, "the cloud over the Holy of Holies," came to a stop, the shrine was assembled; when the sign came to proceed, it was taken down. These tasks were performed by the Levites, the priestly tribe alone permitted to handle the sacred components. When dismantled in the prescribed order, the parts were loaded into the wagons assigned to take them from place to place on the way to the eventual destination, the Promised Land.

The biblical measurements are given in cubits. The cubit, measuring the length of the arm from the end of the middle finger to the elbow, is approximately twenty inches long; the Tabernacle, then, was roughly forty-five feet in length and fifteen feet in width and height. It was made of forty-eight boards of shittim wood (acacia) overlaid on both sides with gold. The boards were joined and made firm by ring links, pegs, and golden bars, five of these to each wall. An intricate system of silver sockets and tenons connected to the baseboards gave the structure an extraordinary flexibility and strength against the uneven ground conditions of the wilderness campsites.

The Tabernacle was divided into the sanctuary (thirty feet long, fifteen wide) and the Holy of Holies, which was fifteen feet square. The two parts were separated from each other by a veil of magnificent tapestry, finely woven and exquisitely designed and embroidered with eagles on one side, lions on the other. It was made of twined linen, blue, purple, and scarlet strands interlaced with strips of thin gold. Four golden pillars held it erect.

The Holy of Holies measured ten cubits by ten cubits by ten cubits—a perfect cube of gold which is the symbol of light, strength, perfection, permanence, and the soul of man. The only object housed in its darkness was the Ark of the Testimony, an oblong chest of acacia wood, overlaid within and without with pure gold, crowned with a molding of fine workmanship, and provided with four golden rings through which two staves were run, so that it was always ready, when the need arose, to be taken out of the Holy of Holies without human touch.

The Ark contained the tablets of testimony (the Ten Commandments), a pot of manna (the sustenance of man in the wilderness), and Aaron's rod. On top of the Ark rested a slab of pure gold, called the "mercy seat," with cherubim of fine gold at either end. The faces of the cherubim turned toward the mercy seat, the dwelling place of the Divine Presence.

In the north of the sanctuary stood a table holding twelve loaves of specially baked bread which were replaced every seventh day. In the south stood the great seven-branched candelabrum, beaten out of a solid piece of pure gold. Oil for its light was prepared meticulously, according to divine instruction:

only olives from the top of the tree could be used, and from each of these, only the first drop.

In the middle of the sanctuary stood the altar, made of acacia with gold overlay. Incense of an exact preparation, "after the art of the apothecary," and reserved for sacred use, was burned there each morning and evening. The entire sanctuary was covered with a tapestry of all the colors of the rainbow, golden clasps, and interlacings sparkling like the stars in the light of the candelabrum. This was covered by a layer of spun goats' hair, then a layer of rams' wool dyed red, and, finally, a layer of badgers' skins. Thus the inner treasure, its radiance and energy, was protected from the wilderness and unfriendly eyes by swathings of animal hides.

According to tradition, throughout the entire journey through the wilderness, the Ark, the Divine Presence, accompanied the people, leading the way and issuing two fiery beams that burned all snakes, scorpions, and other harmful things in their path. It is said that on entering the Promised Land, the Ark dried up the Jordan River so the Israelites could enter and that it effected the fall of Jericho when it was carried around the walls of the city seven times to the accompaniment of a blast on the rams' horn trumpets till the walls of resistance tumbled down. In the great battles the Ark was brought time and time again to the front. At last, in the temple built by Solomon, the Ark was placed in the Holy of Holies, and the practice of taking it from its shrine ceased altogether.

The ultimate fate of the Ark is obscure. It is not mentioned among the vessels that were carried by the captive Israelites to Babylon or were brought back from that exile. According to one legend, the prophet Jeremiah buried it on Mount Nebo, where Moses viewed the Promised Land and later died. In the Talmudic period, there was a story that prior to the destruction of the First Temple, Solomon in his foresight had prepared subterranean passages to a cave under the Holy of Holies, and that the Ark had been placed there. The few who set out with impure motives to search for it were said to have been struck dead as they approached the site.

Midrashic sources say that the ancient Tabernacle corresponds to the entire universe and to man, who is a small universe. So the Lord informed the apprehensive Moses: "Just as I created the world and your body, you shall make the tabernacle." And indeed, the measure of the pattern of the Tabernacle, its symmetry and proportions, strongly suggest the human body. Studying afresh the instructions for its design and construction, it is striking how applicable they are to the making of a man.

The Tabernacle, built to be the container of the "indwelling divine nature" which is the Ark, indicates the original purpose of all craft—the making of a dwelling place for a higher presence. In its design and the details of its construction is embodied a knowledge of the universe and man's place in it; man is instructed here to build within his body a sanctuary in the wilderness of his daily existence, voluntarily giving of his available materials and abilities for that purpose, working to link his "base minerals" with his finest faculties, his attention, and his aspiration.

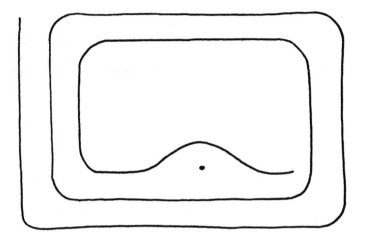

"Your Majesty," said the carpenter, "what you call magic comes only from what I have already told you."

X: *THE HOUSE AS CENTER*

The order of a man's life is this: he is created; he builds a house for himself; he learns how to live in the house. This is the beginning and end of the work.

He is created.

This morning he begins to build. In the clear light, the materials make a pattern on the ground. They come from the ground—the bricks from clay, the concrete blocks from powdered stones and sand, the wood from trees, the nails from iron ores. He cuts the earth below the depth of the frost and lays the foundation in long straight lines. His trowel works ceaselessly between the blocks, skimming the edges of the joints, smoothing the wet cement, tapping the blocks into place. A tight cord between two posts, like a line on a blueprint, guides the straightness of the wall. He builds the corners first, where two walls meet, aligning the blocks in both directions, and then lays the walls to meet the corners. The foundation rises, block upon block, level and true. It appears above the surface of the ground and, when adequately above, it ends.

Thus is the house begun.

The sills rest flat on the foundation walls. The main beam spans the center of the house, with posts under it to support the weight. He lays the floor joists across the beam, braces the joists for rigidity, and nails headers across their outer ends as a support for the walls to come. The frame grows under the action of the saw and hammer, the rule and level, the plumb and square. Where the wood is warped, he pulls it into place. He makes the joints quickly and without haste; they sit firm and tight above each other. Section by section, the walls arise. He places windows so he can see and doors so he can go everywhere. Like sinews in his body, the parts of the frame will brace against its weight, against the push of the wind, against stretching in summer and shrinking in winter. The frame exceeds the height of the sides and reaches the roof. With panels or boards he sheathes the frame in its first covering. When the house is thus enclosed, he nails a bush or a branch from a tree to the highest part of the roof. Then he stops his work and looks at what has been accomplished. What is this celebration of enclosure that calls for a gift from the ground?

As he was created, so must he create. His need for enclosure is instinctive, primordial. It comes from builders before him, from generations of villages, from all races and times. Wherever he builds, an achievement is shared. No craft is more communal than building a house.

The house is an archetype of what he is and of what he can become. Just as walls become high and fire lights a hearth, a transformation can take place within the man. As he transforms, so may he, by the process, be transformed. This is the nature of building, of work in a craft.

His responsibility to build does not end until the house is finished. He must put on the shingles and siding, build the chimney and prepare the rooms. Only then can he move in. Then he will find a new responsibility. The life of the house depends on the inner movements.

At every level, the house knows the secret of its construction. Each section supports the next. The wall rests on the floor, the floor on the walls below it. The house is built by repetitions; so great a task could not be met in any other way. Yet, even as he builds, the house begins to wear. It will be struck by wind and rain, pressed on by snow. It moves toward the ground in a way that he could not foresee.

This morning the house is done, the chimney smooth, the paint polished. The man enters it and takes possession. Thus is completion the way to a beginning.

Within the house, a corridor ascends. It is the line of the chimney, the route of the stair, the high hall beneath the beams. The man climbs the stair. The rail curves upward as smoke in the chimney curls upward. He pursues the steps to the topmost rooms. His window eyes see all around, yet he tries to be unattached to what he sees. His life will be formed around such a rising, in a passageway between the floors.

By such a movement is his work accomplished. The energy that moves is the life in him—in his head, his heart, his hands. As the house will become his house, so will his body be a place for the life within it. When he enters this house, he enters a symbol of himself.

A symbol of himself. Piece upon piece, the inner framework grows, but the result will not be seen until the first enclosure. Yet the supports are as sure as any scaffolding. Much earnest effort is required:

> The Props assist the House
> Until the House is built
> And then the Props withdraw
> And adequate, erect,
> The House support itself
> And cease to recollect
> The Auger and the Carpenter—
> Just such a retrospect
> Hath the perfected Life—
> A past of Plank and Nail
> And slowness—then the Scaffolds drop
> Affirming it a Soul.[1]

The rooms will be filled in their proper times. What will he bring to them that they require? To find this out will take a lot of living in the house. He will grow as he learns to fill these empty rooms.

How small these rooms seem when they are empty. There is nothing in them to hold the attention. Yet the attention is held; it does not go outside. Something arises here, something exists, that seems to come from emptiness. Something is present, diffuse and waiting, that is a center in the room. It is not a geometric center but a center of a different kind. It comes and goes, but still it stays. Its power is simple and not commanding. It is the source, the beginning, of what is possible in the room.

The house is formed, made living around these centers. In the same way, something is transformed inside the man. He interprets, creates, builds, each time anew. Always a source, a beginning, exists. His work will grow in this firm and fertile ground.

The work of the man and his family transforms the house in ways unknown to the protecting shell. Life flows from floor to floor, between the rooms; the stair, the hall are vessels for this flow. The family works to find and the rooms come to know their common functioning. Such is the life of a house, within the house. At times, the centers in the house appear to be everywhere, wherever there is a pause in the flow, wherever the members of the family bring to each other or to their work their vital questioning. Centers occur in the work itself: where the nail is driven in, where the needle goes through, where the page receives its mark. On their individual scales, the parts of the house become like that which can be held in the hand.

What properties of a room affect the center? So much of a craft is in this question. The center arises from the emptiness in the room. As the room expands, as things are brought into it, the center moves. Activity begins. What was diffuse when the room was empty appears in places within the room. Thus the room has many centers, yet they belong to one. The centers are places of rest. At every moment they are surrounded by the functioning of the room. The room expands, in this way is established. The craft begins from empty spaces.

As the wood accepts nails, as cloth is sewn and the page is filled, so the house is crafted from its centers.

By such a crafting, the house becomes an enclosure. The house without, the family within, achieve a common completion. The house is made complete by what it holds inside.

The house is able to contain, by reason of this completeness. Two worlds are separated by the thinnest shell. Whether the shell is of stone or wood, grass or the hides of animals, its purpose is the same. All influences creep around it, but they remain outside.

The house as enclosure is the prototype of buildings. It is the father of buildings, the container of crafts. So much of the world is sampled here, so much attempted, so much fulfilled. The family carried in their supplies by the armfuls. They brought logs for the fire, and iron kettles; wood and nails and bolts of cloth. They brought saws and axes, brushes and pencils, scissors and knives. They were painters, poets, spinners, weavers, carpenters, and smiths. They worked at tables and benches, at easels, anvils, and desks. From basement to attic their tools could be found—in cupboards, on walls, in their hands. Some they invented; the thoughts for these woke them at night. It is difficult to tell the true extent of this house.

Skills were taught by a kind of knowledge that passed outward from one member of the family to others in the room. The girl learned how to spin simply by handing the carded wool to the spinner, again and again, and by much watching. The boy learned to saw wood by holding the ends of the wood for another member of the family, again and again, and by much watching. By this means, quite private to themselves, they learned that in the repetition of that which is never quite the same, a possibility is enacted. Such learning was part of the formation of a center.

After work, what stories were read or told here? What lamps were lighted, around what tables did the family gather with their friends? What graces were said, what dishes of food admired? What ceremonies were conducted here? When people come together with care for their gathering, and with such purpose that they learn new meanings, can this not be called a ceremony?

The day of a family is a moment in the life of a building. Does this not mean that the center re-creates itself each moment?

Other places served them—the school, the church, the hospital, the theater—yet to this house they returned. As the house was their shelter, so they were the living center in the house. When they were away on errands, some part of their presence seemed to stay in the house. In such a manner, the center goes and stays.

For the house to grow, a man must live and work here. Then there will be the differences between the rooms, and they will be used for the purposes which their spaces make proper. Is it not the same for the spaces within ourselves? Who will come to live within?

This is the law of the house; upon the top of the mountain the whole limit thereof round about shall be most holy. Behold, this is the law of the house.

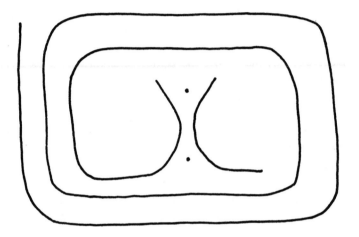

XI: *THE ALCHEMY OF CRAFT*

It is a very old belief (and who is to say that it has entirely disappeared, or that it is entirely mistaken?) that the process of creation is evolutionary growth: the bringing to perfection of all that is created, including matter and including man. God's intention, in other words, and the obedient tendency of nature, is toward "maturity," or perfection. In ancient times, metal ores were thought to be embryos of metals that would in time become gold, which (as the makers of the Tabernacle knew) is the most perfect of all metals, the metal of immortality and of the Sun. "Lead and other metals would become gold if they had time," says Subtle in Ben Jonson's play *The Alchemist*. Left to themselves, in the course of countless thousands of years, ores would grow into metals, and metals into gold; but with fire the metal worker could accomplish in hours what would take nature so many centuries; he could "transform" ores by smelting and change the character of metals. And by so doing, he himself was changed and took on the character of one set apart: a magician, a wielder of power, a collaborator with the Creator. In recognition of this, corresponding qualities were expected of him, and he had to obey certain disciplines. The alchemist "must be healthy, humble, patient, chaste; his mind must be free and in harmony with his work; he must be

intelligent and scholarly, he must work, meditate, pray . . ."[1]
And even today, in Africa, we are told that "the artisan who
works the gold must first of all purify himself, must wash himself from head to foot, and during the time of the work, must
abstain from sexual intercourse."[2]

The gold of alchemy was just this hastened perfection, inner
and outer, the divinization of matter and of man. It would be
as foolish to consider alchemy merely the "pseudo science" of
making gold out of base metals as to suppose that the whole
aim of craft is simply the production of objects, however beautiful. All serious students of alchemy stress that the "Great
Work" was basically that of inner transformation; but the process of a concrete transmutation outside oneself, the actual
transmutation of metals, was a necessary part of the inner process. Alchemy was not simply symbolical. The attempt to bring
metals to the perfection of gold was a vital exercise, at once a
cause and a result, of the inner perfecting. This idea is certainly
not strange to any craftsman. "When a man undertakes to
create something," wrote Paracelsus, "he establishes a new
heaven, as it were, and from it the work that he desires to
create flows into him." In order that it may be expressed, that it
may resound, the Word must be made flesh; immortality must
be incarnated outwardly in gold and inwardly in the development of a subtle body within this ordinary body: the "glorious
body," or "diamond body" of oriental tradition, the "spiritual
body" of the Christian.* The alchemists equated this glorious
body with the Philosopher's Stone of a hundred names—the
elixir, the tincture, the quintessence—and their striving was to
acquire it before the death of the physical body, in this life and
not at the last trump. Man as well as nature could be saved
from the long wait through aeons of time, and the risk of disap-
pearance in the slow cycles of nature, by his own activity, "the

---

* "It is sown a natural body; it is raised a spiritual body." St. Paul in
I Corinthians 15:44.

Great Work." This was his part in the endless march of creation, and his possible "doing" and "making."

The alchemical process, then, was an accelerated version of the process of creation. And here we enter deep waters; for how can we examine anything so huge as the "process of creation" of which we ourselves are so small a part, or anything so vague as the alchemical process which has never been described twice in the same way? But then, we are already in the gravest of difficulties by our very attempt to face the mystery of the possibilities of our own "doing" and "making." And in any case, it is only those who are willing to plunge into water over their heads who will ever try to understand what it is to become true craftsmen, let alone alchemists—those amazingly brave apprentices of a craft which had no known masters, a craft never surely proved to have produced a positive result and which often exposed its followers to scorn, persecution, and ruin. Working in darkness and in secret, it is no wonder that the descriptions they gave of the alchemical process are not only obscure but contradictory. Nevertheless, we can perhaps recognize a pattern and see in it reflections of the ancient analogies of the creation myths.

In Genesis, for example, out of the chaos of undifferentiated matter, God brings order by distinguishing and separating the elements: light and darkness; sea, land, and sky; solid, liquid, and gaseous. And the differentiation continues: animal and plant, then in all its details each form of life "after his kind," and man, and woman. Only then, when everything is distinct and separated from every other thing, can a new order be established and the opposites come together again in a new relationship, man with woman, human with animal and plant. "It is as if spirit and soul had to be separated from one another in order, after their 'divorce,' to become 'married' again."[3] A law of creation seems to appear: the substances must be sorted out, separated, and opposed, in order to connect again in a new way

—as, in individual beings, the differentiation of sex becomes
more and more precise before the opposite poles can unite for
a new generation.

In spite of the varying descriptions of the alchemical process,
we can see that it begins—and, in a way, ends—with something
like a "distillation." The mixed substances in the crucible are
submitted to a long process by fire and then separated into four
substances, or four elements: a "liquid" (Water), an "oil"
(Air), a "mineral" (Earth), and a "tincture" (Fire), with their
different qualities of "dryness," "moisture," "cold," and "heat."
But at first, each element has mixed qualities—"Water," for instance, is cold and moist, "Air" hot and moist—and they must
pass through succeeding distillations until each is purely of one
quality. "Water" must become pure "cold," "Air" wholly
"moist," "Earth" only "dry." The distillation of the "Tincture"
into pure heat is the last step before the final goal is reached,
for as the divine element comes into its own, all four are fused
and in their holy union disappear, to be reborn as the "Fifth,"
or Quintessence—another name for the Philosopher's Stone, the
direct agent of transmutation. "The last (the tincture) seems to
have been the precursor of the Philosopher's Stone," writes
Sherwood Taylor, "being described as a transparent body,
brilliant, lustrous and red. It was presumably that which was
lacking in base metals and present in gold."[4] And yet, out of
base metals it must somehow appear.

"Separate earth from fire, and the subtle from the gross,
softly and with great care," say the Emerald Tablets of Tris-
megistus. Other more detailed accounts of the process indicate
how the original substances in the alchemist's crucible must be
dissolved and reprojected into new formations, each time more
pure and more separated, until at last they come together as
two opposites rather than four: the male and female principles,
the "above" and "below," Sun and Moon, represented in al-

chemy by Sulphur and Mercury. These may then be joined in the fiery bath of the crucible in the "marriage of the King and Queen." The conjunction of the two results in a substance which turns black—the *nigredo,* or "Death." On the next trial by fire this becomes white—the *albedo,* or the "making of the White Stone," the rebirth into silver, and the end of the first stage of the Work. Six more steps are necessary (some say!) for the white stone to turn into the red stone—the quintessence, or Philosopher's Stone—which, applied to heated mercury, turns it into gold.

For the alchemists, the heat which transforms materials in the crucible consists of three parts: the heat of the fire, that residing in the ash bed, and that which is latent in the material itself. It is the latent heat that contains the great possibility for the substance that is to be transformed, for this heat can become active in its own right, and indeed it is the aim of alchemy to activate it. According to Titus Burckhardt, the outer fire "corresponds to the generative power, which is first aroused and then tamed in order to serve inward contemplation . . . The indirect warmth of the ash pit . . . signifies the concentration of the soul, which is indirectly brought about and maintained by the 'open' fire," and the warmth in the enclosed material, which "has to be awakened, is a symbol of the most inward vital force."[5]

However differently the process is described by different students of alchemy, certain principles emerge, which are recognizable as belonging to all processes of transformation, big or small, psychic or physical. As these principles become clear, the different descriptions become less contradictory and more analogous, and alchemy, even in its operational aspect, ceases to be a strange superstition of a past epoch and speaks quite practically of man the maker, the apprentice craftsman, myself. "To make gold, one must have gold," was an alchemistic aphorism;

and Thomas Vaughan says of the "tincture," or "fire,"† that "it
is in minerals, herbs and beasts; it is in man, stars and angels;
but originally it is in God Himself."⁶ We cannot think of creation, even that small creation of our own handiwork, without
fire of both kinds: that of the kiln, the dyeing vat, the forge,
and the inner fire of feeling and of vision, represented by the
sun-gold of light, heat, and the "solar" plexus—the traditional
seat of human feeling—without which nothing beautiful can be
made. The alchemical paradoxes of the "volatilization of the
solid and the solidification of the volatile" and of "burning
water and liquid fire" are quite understandable for the artist
who acknowledges that to produce true art, he himself must be
changed and come to a finer state: a "spiritualization of the
body," the instrument, before there can be an "embodiment of
the spirit."

This "becoming" is what alchemy is about. Its process can
also be expressed by the traditional formulas of initiation: the
suffering, death, and resurrection of the god or the neophyte,
represented by the substances in the crucible or by the material
of the craftsman—the symbolic formula of transformation.
Osiris, the divine craftsman of the Egyptians, is slain by his
brother and his body is dismembered and scattered; but he lives
again to beget Horus and to become the king of the dead.
Quetzalcoatl sacrifices himself in the fire to atone for the sins of
the body and is resurrected as the morning star; the twin heroes
of the Popol Vuh leap together into the bonfire prepared by
the enemy gods, but rise from their ashes and conquer the Underworld. And, following these divine examples, candidates for
initiation suffer tortures and ritual death in order to attain another state of being. In each case, whether raw material, base
metal, divine or human spirit, there must be the suffering of

† Fire, gold, the sun, sulphur, and the male (creative) principle are closely
identified in alchemical symbolism.

purification and separation. The patience that has been spoken
about in earlier chapters as the quality most vital to the craftsman is, in the final analysis, no other than this suffering, as it
applies to the process of creation operating in and upon the artisan himself.‡ And as the alchemical substance is "punished,"
so is the craftsman's material: clay is pounded; flax beaten;
wool teased, carded, and twisted; metal softened and struck.
The substance, whether material or human, must change its
character, be torn into separate elements in order to be re-
formed into something other—it must "die" in order to be
"reborn."

And here we come to the central tenet of alchemy: its chief
absurdity, proof (some would say) that in its operational sense
at least it was all superstition and quackery; the idea that matter is alive. Yet, strangely enough, this is something that every
craftsman knows to be true. He knows that his material has a
life of its own, a history, a character, needs, and possibilities
unlike any other. He knows that he must feel and understand
this life so that a relationship can appear between it and his
own. He accepts a pattern for his work that is not "his," that
comes to him, as it were, from above; but his work is not
merely to obey and to imitate, nor even only to "speed the
process of nature," but to bring something peculiarly his,
some element of himself, to unite with that other living entity,
the material between his hands. Otherwise the relation does not
exist; the material is indeed dead, and he himself no more than
a copyist. The gold of the alchemist was not the same as
natural gold; it was "living" gold. He added something even
to the noblest of metals by his active relation with it.

Perhaps we could paraphrase what Coomaraswamy has written of art and religion and say that craft is alchemy, alchemy
craft, not related, but the same. For the craftsman, as well as

‡ Latin *patiens,* from *pati,* to suffer.

the alchemist, knows that his central task is the creation of himself; and it is above all for this aim that he strives with endless patience, separating "the subtle from the gross, softly and with great care," to make what his hands touch turn to gold.

EPILOGUE: THE FOOTFALL OF A CAT

There is no traditional game . . . , nor any kind of fairy tale
properly to be so called (excepting, that is to say, those which
merely reflect the fancies of individual literateurs, a purely modern phenomenon) nor any sort of traditional jugglery, that is not
at the same time that it is an entertainment, the embodiment of a
metaphysical doctrine.

A. K. Coomaraswamy[1]

Let us go back to the beginning of this book and remember
that it was Chuang Tzü's story of the carpenter that gave us a
direction and a form. For writing is itself a craft, and story and
myth are among craft's handmaidens. If we go back to the real
beginning, as all stories must—what else does "Once upon a
time" mean?—to the making of the universe, Genesis tells us
that God made "every flower of the field before it was in the
earth, and every herb of the field before it grew," cribbing
thereby from Plato, who was not yet either born or had thought
of—past and future in eternity being interchangeable—the
Theory of Ideas. So, out of no-thing—or Mind, if you like—
the Great Craftsman, expressing what had to be expressed, like
all his crafts-sons after him, fashioned his mighty artifacts.

"Tyger, Tyger burning bright, In the forests of the night: What immortal hand or eye, Dare frame thy fearful symmetry?"

And so, once man was eventually in being, the craftsman—not, you will notice, the artist—inevitably abounded. Speaking historically, the word "artist" is a comparatively modern invention. Noah would not have called himself an artist; he built according to instructions from within—and within is here and always synonymous with above—his famous ark which is so embedded in human memory that it is now one with the fairy tales. Properly brought-up children are as familiar with raven, dove, and olive branch as they are with Rumpelstiltskin. The theme has even dwindled into a popular song:

> The animals went in one by one,
> There's one more river to cross.
> The elephant eating a caraway bun,
> There's one more river to cross.
>
> One more river,
> And that's the river of Jordan,
> One more river,
> There's one more river to cross.

And what toy cupboard is complete without the clumsy, homely, wooden structure—"Make thee an ark of gopher wood . . . A window shalt thou make to the ark . . . and the door of the ark shalt thou set in the side thereof"—looking rather like the Peggotty houseboat in *David Copperfield?*

And Hiram of Tyre, king and artisan—the two callings were in those days not incompatible—to whom Solomon entrusted a large part of the building of the Temple—the cherubim and the palm trees "with gold fitted upon the carved work," the pillars, the pomegranates—did he assume the name of artist? Did Phidias? Or the builders of the Gothic cathedrals?

The artificer, the smith, the maker have always been given a high, even aristocratic place in traditional cultures. The Scots have immemorially called their balladists *makars,* which has the same meaning as the Greek *poiētēs,* or maker. The smith, the worker in iron or metal, and this includes the blacksmith, the fettler, maker of horseshoes and harness buckles (remember Felix Randal, who as Gerard Manley Hopkins wrote, "fettle[d] for the great grey drayhorse his bright and battering sandal") —think of all these and their lofty station in myth, legend, and fairy tale. It was Culain, the smith, who was instrumental in setting the boy Setanta on his way to being the chief hero-figure of Irish story. Setanta had come late to the feast given by the smith for the High King and his court and encountered the ferocious wolfhound (*cu*) which had been set to guard the fortress. The tremendous baying of the hound brought the feasting concourse to the gates only to find a young lad tearing the animal's mighty jaws apart and flinging the corpse to the ground.

"Boy!" cried Culain, "thou hast slain my guard. How shall I fare for protection?" "Give me, O Culain, a whelp of that hound and I will train him to be more potent than his sire. Till then, let you give me shield and spear and I myself will be your guard. Henceforth, I am no longer Setanta but Cuculain, the hound of the smith." And it is under that name that he reigns in legend.

Hephaistos, the god of artificers, was the son of Hera, the spouse of Zeus. At Hephaistos' birth, because he was a weakling, Hera incontinently flung him into the sea. Thence he was rescued by the goddesses Thetis and Eurynome and kept in a grotto for nine years until he had learned the art of working in metal. From there Hera, with her all-seeing goddess eye, perceiving the excellence of his workmanship, again incontinently plucked him and set him up in a workshop on Mount Olympus where he became known as the smith god. Homer tells us that he fashioned twelve golden mechanical women to help him in his labors. But it was he alone, for love of his foster-mother Thetis, who fashioned the armor for her son, Achilles, of which this story tells us:

Now, Thetis of the silver feet came to the house of Hephaistos, the smith, and found him working at his forge. "Noblest of immortals!" he exclaimed. "You who spread out arms to save me when my mother, because I was lame at birth, flung me into the sea; you who, with Eurynome, reared me in a cave where I learned my cunning and curious craft—fashioning necklaces, brooches, rings—while the surging ocean foamed about me; you who eased my suffering soul, welcome to my house!" He limped toward her among the wheeling tripods and the golden, almost-human handmaids and took her by the hand. "Tell me what it is you desire and I will be swift to do it!"

Then Thetis, weeping, begged him to fashion for her son, Achilles, a new and matchless suit of armor—helmet, shield, cuirass, and greaves—to replace the original harness lost at the siege of Troy.

"Weep not, goddess," cried Hephaistos. "To save your son from the power of death, I will make him armor that will rejoice his heart and fill all mortals with wonder."

So saying, he set the bellows to the fire and grasped his hammer and tongs. First he made a shield, five-layered and with a triple rim. And on it he wrought the earth and the sea, the tireless sun and moon in the sky, and all the constellations. Beneath the heavens lay two mortal cities—one all bright with festival; brides led by torchlight from their maiden chambers; young men circling in the dance; crowds assembling in the market place to discuss the blood price of a murdered man; heralds keeping all in order; elders sitting in judgment.

But the second city showed forth war, besieged as it was by two armies. Women, children, and old men sheltered within the walls, while without, the warriors lay in ambush where the countrymen herded their cattle. Slaughter was everywhere; the struggle for bodies, weapons, and armor; hate and confusion. But as well there was tilled and fruitful land, triple-plowed by teams of plowmen to whom would be handed flagons of wine as they turned at the end of the furrow.

To the tilled land Hephaistos added a vineyard, fit for any king's precinct, with golden grapes hanging from branches of silver. Young men and maidens bore the fruit away, dancing to the music of a youth with a lyre. Cattle fashioned of gold and tin pastured beside a river, herded by shepherds and hounds of gold. Two lions bounded into the scene, seizing one of the foremost bullocks amid the baying hounds. And beyond these lay a quiet valley, grazed by a flock of silver sheep. Among its folds and shepherds' houses a chain of youths and maidens danced, girls with wreaths upon their heads, young men with golden daggers. Tumblers whirled to the tune of a harp and countrymen crowded to the festival. And around all these scenes in gold and silver, out at the uttermost rim of the circle the great river Oceanus flowed like a shining serpent.

When the smith of Olympus had finished the shield, he forged a breastplate brighter than fire, a helmet crowned with a crest of gold, cuirass and greaves of tin. Then Hephaistos of the strong arms lifted the mighty works of his hands and laid them before the mother of Achilles.

And Thetis, as a hawk its prey, seized upon the golden armor and swept down from the snows of Olympus, bearing to the earth and her son the shining gift of Heaven.[2]

Was it some memory of Hephaistos, tellurian, common to all men, or because of the universality of the motifs of myth, that tribes in Africa, Asia, Indo-Europe, deliberately lamed their smiths lest they abscond to other tribes with all their ancient expertise? Legend, of course, does not explain. To explain is not its function. Nevertheless, the theme of laming is a sign of the smith's hero-place in the cultures of the past.

We meet the theme of the smith again—though this time whole of limb—in the great epic of Finland, the *Kalevala*, with Ilmarinen, the wonder-smith, "who invented iron" and fashioned the enchanted Samppo, which was at once flour mill, salt mill, coin mill, *and* world axis, giver of all good, spindle of the universe. Ilmarinen, however, in spite of the fact that he forges the hero's weapons, is a supernumerary in our next story which deals, in effect, with two other crafts—that of words, not as poetry but as power, and, as a result of discovering these, of shipbuilding, albeit of a magic kind. Before our craft theme begins, the hero, Väinämöinen, has fallen helplessly in love with the Maiden of Pohjala. And inevitably, since we have to have a story, we come upon an obstacle. Her mother, who was a witch, demanded as her daughter's dowry an enchanted ship that was to be built from stem to stern entirely without hands. So Väinämöinen, warrior as well as smith, set himself to the task. He found, however, that to complete the vessel he needed to know Three Words of Power. Through the world he therefore sought them, exploring even the realms of Death, but always without success. At length he met a shepherd who advised him that the only way to discover the Lost Sayings was from the mouth of the giant wizard, Vipunen, who had been dead—or sleeping—for aeons.

So Väinämöinen, journeying over "the points of needles and the edges of broadswords and the sharpened blades of hatchets," came at last to the resting place of the magician from whose great body grew alder, birch, willow, and oak. These the smith swiftly felled and, thrusting his staff of iron through the mouth of Vipunen, pried the mighty jaws asunder.

"Rise," he cried, "thou great magician, from thine everlasting slumber!"

Then Vipunen uttered a howl of anguish and opened his

mouth so wide that Väinämöinen fell headlong into it. There he was, deep in the body of the giant—like Jonah in the belly of the whale—and there, he decided, he would stay until he had achieved his quest.

From the handle of his dagger he made a well-proportioned boat in which he rowed through the entrails of Vipunen; from his armor he made a smithy; from his sleeves he contrived the bellows; from his knees he made an anvil and a hammer of his forearm; and with these he went to work.

At long last Vipunen protested. With threats and curses he adjured Väinämöinen to leave him, calling down upon him all the powers of evil and destruction. But the hero, bent upon his aim, was not to be deterred. Summoning all his force of will, he challenged his mighty host, vowing not to depart before learning his wisdom-sayings.

At that, Vipunen, recognizing that he was in the presence of one worthy to receive it, opened up his store of knowledge and for three days without ceasing sang the ancient incantations and the lordly words of power. The story tells how, along with Väinämöinen, the stars themselves harkened to this singing; the moon stood still to listen; tides of ocean stopped their courses and the Jordan ceased from flowing. And when Väinämöinen had heard the missing runes to the end, he prepared himself to leave the body that had housed him for so long. Vipunen blessed him and let him go. And Väinämöinen, armed with the mythic words of power, returned to his own land and built and launched his ship.

So, by means of the lost sayings, the great task was accomplished.[3]

From the deeps of the wizard, or, symbolically, from his own depths, the hero, like every other craftsman after him, discovers at once his way and what the way expresses. There is an echo here of Jonah's night journey in the Old Testament. It cannot

be said that Jonah was, in any sense that is relevant to the
theme of this book, a craftsman. We cannot include his story
here. Yet the same alchemical process is at work as with
Väinämöinen, the willingness to explore the dark—inner or
outer, it doesn't matter—in order to find the light. The Har-
rowing of Hell must take place before we can hope to look for
Heaven. Every craftsman is familiar with this experience.

So much for the epics. When we come to the fairy tales, we
find that they seldom deal specifically with any craft, though
the symbolical craft of man fashioning himself is always to the
fore. True, the tales deal with laboring folk: the father of Han-
sel and Gretel was a woodcutter; the Cunning Little Tailor,
though no worker himself, had two companions who plied their
needles dexterously; the Three Army Surgeons could cut off a
leg with great precision and provide a salve for any wound; the
Four Skillful Brothers excelled in their professions—one as a
thief, one as an astronomer, one as a huntsman, one as a
weaver; Allerleirauh, temporarily of course, since she was a
princess in disguise, was an exemplary kitchenmaid; Long-Lip,
Swell-Thumb, and Spade-Foot gave so much time to their spin-
ning that, as their names record, they grossly distorted their
bodies. But none of these were craftsmen in our sense; they
practiced their callings by the way, their trades were never the
nub of the story. One can, I think, make an exception of *The
Adventures of Pinocchio,* a comparatively modern fairy tale,
where Geppetto, an old wood carver, hears a piece of timber
laughing and speaking. There is something true here. The pot
calls to the potter from the clay, the figure calls to the
stonemason from the marble. Geppetto answers the call of the
wood and presently there is a puppet. And ultimately, through
his own suffering and self-searching—he too goes on a night
journey in the belly of the dogfish—his puppet becomes a real
boy. Any craftsman, reading the story on a level other than that
on which it is written, is bound to find in himself an aspect of

Geppetto. Unwittingly, seeking only to amuse, Carlo Collodi, the author of *Pinocchio,* happened upon a theme that he did not clearly understand and one that was older than he knew. Indeed, craft themes are always old. In this, as in many other ways, modern man lives on the fat of his ancestors. Even the following excerpts from *Her-Bak,* written in this century by Isha Schwaller de Lubicz, came to us from a very remote past. In the Egyptian studies which she shared with her distinguished husband and their long work of delving into the symbolism of the hieroglyphs, an ancient system of thought was uncovered which she embodied in the story of the boy Her-Bak—otherwise Chick-Pea, or Face-of-Horus—who grows from childhood to manhood within the precincts of the Temple. On his way from the outer Temple, or peristyle, to the inner courts, he is inevitably inducted into various crafts. By "temple" we are to understand not merely the whole structure of Egyptian science, as discovered at Karnak, but the living temple of man himself —*le temple dans l'homme*—who, as microcosm, personifies the principles and functions of the macrocosm. Our excerpt shows the boy submitting himself, a willing apprentice, to the material in which he works and at the same time to his own transformation:

THE JOINER*

> One evening, weary of trying without success to fit a tenon into a slot, Chick-Pea nevertheless made up his mind to persevere with it and remained at work when the others went home. With small, precise cuts he busied himself with finishing the adjustment, and as the workshop was empty, he sang in rhythm with his movements . . .

* From *Her-Bak Chick-Pea: The Living Face of Ancient Egypt,* published by and with the permission of Inner Traditions International, New York.

A hand was put on the singer's shoulder . . . Nadjar took the chisel out of his hand, then he led him to the woodstore: roughly squared blocks of carob, ebony and juniper. "Workman," he said, "pay attention to my questions: if you are ripe for higher training, you will have to solve this problem: you have drilled holes into a soft wood: what kind of wood will you have to choose for the pegs so that the adjustment may be durable and solid?"

Chick-Pea touched and looked at the blocks . . . "Is it not true, that if a peg of hard wood enters into soft wood, it may wear it out and at last make it split?"

"That is right. But now, if it is to play freely, as for instance in the case of hinges, so that it is liable to wear and tear, what would you do then?"

"Then I think, one would have to choose the hard wood."

Nadjar put his hand on the anxious head . . . "You have answered well; violence is not a medium of harmony; that is why we adjust wood with wood, and not with metal . . . One must search for the means of making or undoing something always *within its own nature* . . . Now, look at the cut of this trunk: you can read the *medu-Neters* [hieroglyphs]? Can you read the age of this tree in its concentric rings? . . . And do you know why the rib of a palm is the hieroglyph of the year? Do you know that at each New Moon a new frond grows on the date tree?"

. . . "Then our hieroglyphs, and our crafts, and Nature, these are all one and the same science?"

Nadjar's face lit up: "Yes, my son, that is what you were meant to understand . . . As you are going to study our ways of working more thoroughly, it is time to give you a few words of truth: what use you make of them will be your test. Until this day you have been a workman carrying out prescribed movements. The artisan is distinct from the workman because he is aware of his *movement,* of the *instrument,* and of the *material* in which he works. But the accomplished craftsman goes further. He knows the laws of the material and tries to understand their causes. He knows the name of things and their symbolic meaning. That is the Way."

"And this way leads to the Temple?" Chick-Pea asked.

"Who then," Nadjar asked in return, "has drafted and wrought all our temples, statues, symbolic objects, if not the craftsman? And he who knows the causes and the laws, is he not a pillar of the Temple?"

"O, my Master," replied Chick-Pea, "I want to become a craftsman."

"Your way," said Nadjar, "is the right way if you understand this: what you receive depends on what you give; there is what you give the craft, and there is what the craft gives you.

"The *workman* gives the toil of his arm, his energy, his exact or inexact movement; for this the craft gives him a notion of the resistance of the material and its manner of reaction.

"The *artisan* gives the craft his love; and to him the craft responds by making him one with his work.

"But the *craftsman* gives the craft his passionate research into the laws of Nature which govern it; and the craft teaches him Wisdom . . .

"Learn to feel the wood, my son, as you handle your tools, for the wood makes its own demands: all life is not yet quite extinguished in it—whatever the ignorant may think—unless some mistake has been made in cutting it down."

Chick-Pea's curiosity awoke. "Oh, tell me, what are the mistakes that can be made?"

"If you cut a tree after the sap has stopped rising in it, then the fibers will be empty, dead, liable to alteration and deformation in the course of time, through heat or drought."

"And does anyone know what stops the sap from rising?"

"Certain times are known, and certain circumstances; these are the secrets of the observing and 'conscious' craftsman; but one does not speak of this, my son, lest the ignorant scribes should laugh."[4]

We make a mistake when we think of tradition historically, in terms of time. It deals, rather, with other dimensions—"eternity" is not quite the right word but it is as near as we can come to what is, in essence, inexpressible. We can say, perhaps, that there are not so much traditions, as one single tradition. This being so, it is no great step from ancient Egypt to ancient China; we are merely hopping over a neighbor's fence. Our Chinese stories are from the meditations of Chuang Tzü, the great disciple of Lao Tse, who—two hundred years after Lao Tse was last seen riding up into the sky on a buffalo—put into words his master's Wordless Teaching:

> The Tao that can be told of
> Is not the Absolute Tao [Way];
> The Names that can be given
> Are not Absolute Names.
>
> The Nameless is the origin of Heaven and Earth;
> The Named is the Mother of All Things.[5]

Lao Tse's Way was not of knowing but of being, which is inevitably the craftsman's way, if he is truly to be called a craftsman. His manner of doing things and the objects he makes depend, finally, upon what he is. Here, again, in Chuang Tzü, the Cook and the Wheelwright are in no sense below the salt. They are *by no means* without reputation; they consort with Dukes and Princes. And the Dukes and Princes, like the heroes of epic, are content to learn from them. "From the words of this cook," says Prince Hui, "I have learnt how to take care of [or to live] my life." In other words, he recognizes that here he is in the presence of traditional wisdom, the inexhaustible well from which the craftsman of all ages draws his experience.

PRINCE HUI'S EXCELLENT COOK

Prince Hui's cook was cutting up a bullock. Every blow of his hand, every heave of his shoulders, every tread of his foot, every thrust of his knee, every *whahh* of rent flesh, every *chhk* of the chopper, was in perfect harmony—rhythmical like the dance of the Mulberry Grove, simultaneous like the chords of the Ching Shou.

"Well done!" cried the Prince. "Yours is skill indeed."

"Sire," replied the cook, "I have always devoted myself to Tao. It is better than skill. When I first began to cut up bullocks, I saw before me simply whole bullocks. After three years' practice, I saw no more whole animals. And now I work with my mind and not with my eye. When my senses bid me stop, but my mind urges me on, I fall back upon eternal principles. I follow such openings or cavities as there may be, according to the natural constitution of the animal. I do not attempt to cut through joints; still less through large bones.

"A good cook changes his chopper once a year—because he cuts. An ordinary cook, once a month—because he hacks. But I have had this chopper nineteen years, and although I have cut up many thousand bullocks, its edge is as fresh as if new from the whetstone. For at the joints there are always interstices, and the edge of the chopper being without thickness, it remains only to insert that which is without thickness into such an interstice. By these means the interstices will be enlarged, and the blade will find plenty of room. It is thus that I have kept my chopper for nineteen years as though fresh from the grindstone.

"Nevertheless, when I come upon a hard part where the blade meets with a difficulty, I am all caution. I fix my eye on it. I stay my hand and gently apply my blade, until with a *hwah* the part yields like earth crumbling to the ground. Then I take out my chopper, and stand up, and look around, and pause, until with an air of triumph I wipe my chopper and put it carefully away."

"Bravo!" cried the Prince. "From the words of this cook I have learnt how to take care of my life."[6]

DUKE   HWAN   AND   THE   WHEELWRIGHT

Duke Hwan of Khi,
First in his dynasty,
Sat under his canopy,
Reading his philosophy.
Phien the wheelwright
Was out in the yard
Making a wheel.
Phien laid aside
Hammer and chisel,
Climbed the steps
And said to Duke Hwan:
"May I ask you, Lord,
What is this you are
Reading?"
The Duke said:
"The experts. The authorities."
And Phien asked:
"Alive or dead?"
"Dead a long time."
"Then," said the wheelwright,
"You are reading only
The dirt they left behind."
Then the Duke replied:
"What do you know about it?
You are only a wheelwright.
You had better give me a good explanation
Or else you must die."
The wheelwright said:
"Let us look at the affair
From my point of view.
When I make wheels

If I go easy, they fall apart,
If I am too rough, they do not fit.
If I am neither too easy nor too violent
They come out right. The work is what
I want it to be.
You cannot put this into words:
You just have to know how it is.
I cannot even tell my own son exactly how it is done,
And my own son cannot learn it from me.
So here I am, seventy years old,
Still making wheels!
The men of old
Took all they really knew
With them to the grave.
And so, Lord, what you are reading there
Is only the dirt they left behind them."[7]

The Hasidic stories, with their religious overtones, clearly come from the same well of wisdom. Their focal point may indeed be the Baal Shem Tov, whose teaching flourished in the mid-eighteenth century, but they all have the flavor and scent of something cherished and fingered and handed down from a long traditional past. It is true that the rabbi in each story has a name and sometimes a date, but the protagonists are all nameless men, hose-maker or wood-cutter, who have been walking their pilgrim way for unnumbered centuries. Each anecdote shares with the fairy tale its pride, simplicity, and truthfulness.

THE HOSE-MAKER

Once, in the course of a journey, the Baal Shem stopped in a little town whose name has not come down to us. One morning before prayers, he smoked his pipe as usual and looked out of the window. He saw a man go by. This man carried his prayer shawl and phylacteries in his hand and set his feet as intently and solemnly as though he were going straight to the doors of Heaven. The Baal Shem asked the disciple in whose house he was staying, who the man was. He was told that he was a hose-maker who went to the House of Prayer day after day, both summer and winter, and said his prayers even when the prescribed quorum of ten worshippers was not complete. The Baal Shem wanted to have the man brought to him, but his host said: "That fool would not stop on his way—not if the emperor called him in person."

After prayer, the Baal Shem sent someone to the man with the message that he should bring him four pairs of hose. Soon after, the man stood before him and displayed his wares. They were of good sheep's wool and well-made. "What do you want for a pair?" asked Rabbi Israel.

"One and a half gulden."

"I suppose you will be satisfied with one gulden."

"Then I should have said one gulden," the man replied.

The Baal Shem instantly paid him what he had asked. Then he went on questioning him. "How do you spend your days?"

"I ply my trade."

"And how do you ply it?"

"I work until I have forty or fifty pairs of hose. Then I put them into a mould with hot water and press them until they are as they should be."

"And how do you sell them?"

"I don't leave my house. The merchants come to me to buy. They also bring me good wool they have bought for me, and I pay them for their pains. This time I left my house only to honor the rabbi."

"And when you get up in the morning, what do you do before you go to pray?"

"I make hose then, too."

"And what psalms do you recite?"

"I say those psalms which I know by heart, while I work," said the man.

When the hose-maker had gone home, the Baal Shem said to the disciples who stood around him: "Today you have seen the cornerstone which will uphold the Temple until the Messiah comes."[8]

THE PARABLE OF THE WOOD-CUTTER

In his youth Rabbi Zusya joined the congregation of the Great Maggid, Rabbi Baer of Mezritch. But he did not stay with the other disciples. He roamed through the woods, lay down in hidden places, and sang his praises to God, until the people quoted Solomon's words when they spoke to him: "With her love be thou ravished always." His younger brother Elimelekh, who was still a boy and did not as yet belong to the congregation, sat over his books. He wondered at Zusya and once asked him: "Brother, why do you act so that everyone in the House of Study says it is strange?" Zusya answered him with a smile: "My brother, I shall tell you a story." And this is the story:

A poor wood-cutter had a great longing to see the king face to face. So he left his village and walked for many days until he came to the city where the king lived. After trying for a long time, he succeeded in getting employment in the king's palace. He was to tend the stoves. And now he put all the zeal and good sense he was capable of into his work. He went to the forest himself, fetched the best wood, fragrant with resin, split it into even logs, and—at just the right hour—stacked these deftly in the various fireplaces. The king enjoyed the good living warmth. It was better than what he had had, and he asked how this came about. When they told him about the wood-cutter and his work, he sent him a message that he could have a wish. The poor man begged that he might be allowed to see the king every once in a while. His wish was granted. They made a window in a narrow passage which led to the woodshed and this window faced the king's living room, so the wood-cutter could look through and satisfy his longing.

Now once, when the king's son was seated at his father's board, he said something which displeased him and was punished by a year's banishment from the king's apartments. For a time he lived in bitter loneliness. Then he began to wander mournfully through the corridors of the palace. When he came to the little window they had made for the wood-cutter, he was seized with still greater longing to see his father again and begged the man to let him look through. They got to talking together.

"My brother," said Zusya to Elimelekh, when he had reached this point in his story, "this is what the wood-cutter told the prince when they were talking to each other. 'You are at home in the rooms of the lord and eat at his table. All you need do is to govern your speech wisely. But I have neither wisdom nor learning, and so I must perform my lowly service that I may sometimes see the lord's face.' "9

We come now, not to the ending—for tradition has no end—but to the last of our batch of stories. It has been included here because it has in it several elements or threads. There is the component of magic—how else could the metal gold be transformed into human hair?—if, indeed, you can call a goddess human! Again, as so often in the epics, the work itself is done underground, in the innermost part of the craftsman's own earth. And here—a very rare occurrence, this—there are two hero makers: the one who forms and transforms substance, the other who labors bravely on, blowing the bellows—the manual work—while being continually stung by a gadfly. There is a symbolism here that any craftsman will understand. Who isn't perpetually being stung by a gadfly—call it any name you will —while expressing what is to be expressed? But, on second thought, are they really two heroes? Are they not two aspects of one craftsman, the mind in collusion with the hand? Remember that Brok and Sindri are brothers!

There is also the element of the trickster, common to so many stories—the Norse god Loki's boundless gift for mischief, for example. And out of that comes the theme that Shakespeare —scavenging through tradition for his plots—restated in *The Merchant of Venice.* "You may have my head," says Loki to Brok, "but nothing in our bargain allows you to touch my neck." And so his head is saved. Shylock, readying his knife in order to cut off a pound of Antonio's flesh, is halted by Portia.

Tarry a little; there is something else.
This bond doth give thee here no jot of blood!

And, of course, we know the outcome. The epic memory is in our hemoglobin. Shakespeare merely reminds us of it.

One day, when Thor's wife, Sif, was sleeping, Loki the trickster happened to pass by, and because he was in his usual mischievous mood he took some scissors from his pocket and cut off Sif's beautiful golden hair.

When Thor came home and saw what had happened, he was so full of anger that lightning flashed from his two eyes and the palace trembled beneath his feet.

"I know who has done this," he shouted. "It can be none other than that rascal Loki!" And striding off to the palace of Asgard, he seized Loki by the neck and would have strangled him if Loki had not confessed his deed and promised to restore at once Sif's beauty.

So down he went, deep underground, seeking the dwarfs, the sons of Ivald, who were workers in gold and brass and iron.

"Make me a crown of golden hair that will grow upon the head of Sif and I will give you whatever you ask."

And in no time, the busy dwarfs had fashioned a golden

crown for Sif and, in addition, gave to Loki the spear, Gungnir, and the wonderful ship, Skidbladnir.

Loki hurried away to Asgard, boasting of the marvelous treasures he had brought from the sons of Ivald. "No other dwarfs in all the world could have done such work," he boasted.

Now, a dwarf named Brok was standing by, and he called in an angry voice to Loki. "My brother Sindri is a better craftsman than any son of Ivald!"

"If your brother Sindri can make more precious things than these, he can have my head!" said Loki.

"He shall have it, never fear," laughed Brok, and he hurried away to the underworld to tell his brother of the wager.

So the two dwarfs set to work, with Brok blowing the bellows and making the coals a blaze of light and Sindri cleaning a pig's skin and placing it in the furnace.

"Blow till I come back," said Sindri, as he left the smithy to get more coal.

So Brok blew with all his might, taking no notice of a buzzing gadfly that settled on his hand and stung it. And after a while Sindri came back and took out of the furnace a golden boar with bristles that shone in the light.

Then Sindri took a nugget of gold and placed it in the furnace. "Blow for your life!" he said to Brok, and out he went a second time.

The faithful Brok went on with his work and even when the gadfly stung him on the neck, he did not lift his hand from the bellows. And when Sindri came back he took from the fire a golden ring and laid it beside the boar.

Then once more he threw something on the fire. This time it was a lump of iron. "Blow without ceasing," he said to Brok, and he left his brother alone again.

No sooner had he gone than the gadfly settled upon Brok's forehead and stung him so sharply that the blood ran down into both his eyes and he could not see what he was doing. As he raised his hand to brush it away, the bellows ceased to blow. It was at that moment that Sindri returned.

"You have almost spoiled it, brother," he said, as he took from the fire a mighty hammer, still red from the heat of the coals. "The handle is just a trifle short but we cannot alter it now. So take it to Asgard with the boar and the ring and bring me that rascal Loki's head."

In the courts of Asgard the gods entered and took their thrones and waited to see what would come of the contest. Odin, Thor, and Freya were appointed to judge between Loki and Brok and the gifts which each had brought.

Loki stood forth with the spear, Gungnir, which was known never to miss its mark, and presented it to Odin. The golden hair he handed to Thor, who placed it upon the head of Sif where at once it began to grow. And to Freya he gave the ship Skidbladnir which could sail the sea in any breeze and yet could be folded up like paper and carried in a pocket.

Then he turned and scornfully laughed at Brok. "Can that brother of yours do as well as this? Bring out his paltry trinkets!"

Brok stood before the wondering gods, his treasures in his hands.

"This ring," he said, handing it to Odin, "will cast off, every ninth night, eight other rings as fine as itself. This boar," he declared, giving it to Freya, "will run in the air, on the earth and the sea, and no night will be so dark and gloomy that the shining of these golden bristles will not make it as light as noonday. And this hammer"—he placed the hammer, which was to be known as Mjolner, in the hands of Thor—"shall never fail, no matter how hard the thing it smites. Moreover, however far away you throw it, Mjolner will always return to your hand. You may make it as large or as small as you wish and the only fault to be found with it is the shortness of the handle."

Thor swung the hammer around his head and lightning flashed and flamed in Asgard and thunder rolled through the sky. The other gods surrounded him and passed the hammer from one to the other, declaring that from henceforth it would be their greatest protection against their enemies. "Sindri," they said, "has won the wager."

"Then I shall take him Loki's head," said Brok, drawing his sword.

Loki frowned. He had no intention of paying his debt. "I will give you whatever thing you ask, except my head," he growled.

"Your head or nothing!" answered the dwarf.

"Then take it, if you can," cried Loki. But by the time Brok reached the spot where he had been standing, Loki was far away, for he was wearing his famous shoes that could run through the air or over water.

But Thor, who had even swifter shoes, ran after him and brought him back, for the gods always see to it that promises are kept.

"Well, cut off my head," said the cunning Loki. "But the wager gave you no right to my neck. Do not dare to touch it!"

It was true. And Brok knew it. The head could not be taken without wounding the neck. Sindri had lost his chance of revenge.

But Brok determined to get even with Loki. So he took an awl and a leather thong and sewed the trickster's lips together so that he could do no more boasting.

Thus the dwarfs were satisfied and the gods of Asgard were well content.[10]

So the stories repeat themselves in a never-ending gyre, stemming from some ultimate source of which we have no knowledge, only in our instinctive parts a kind of recollection—something wordless that speaks to us of long, continuous processes, of making, remaking, and balancing; the necessity of the gadfly, the identity of the two ends of the spectrum, dark akin to light. Loki, too, it must not be forgotten, was a special kind of craftsman. It was he who fashioned the rope that was to bind the wolf Fenris who, if set free, would forever destroy the world. And of what did he make it?

> The footfall of a cat,
> The roots of a rock,
> The beard of a woman,
> The breath of a fish,
> The spittle of a bird.

So—out of nothing—all; existence from nonexistence. Thus the craftsman, from what in himself is metaphysical makes the tangible physical object.

NOTES

Introduction:

1. A. K. Coomaraswamy, *Christian and Oriental Philosophy of Art* (New York: Dover Publications, 1956).
2. Marie Louise von Franz, *Patterns of Creativity Mirrored in Creation Myths* (Zurich: Spring Publications, 1972).
3. A. K. Coomaraswamy, op. cit.

Chapter I:

1. Simone Weil, *The Need for Roots*, tr. Arthur Will (New York: Harper Torchbook, Harper & Row, 1971).
2. *A Hopkins Reader*, ed. John Pick (New York: Oxford University Press, 1953).
3. Henry Adams, *Mont-Saint-Michel and Chartres* (Boston: Houghton Mifflin, 1933).
4. Henry Adams, *The Education of Henry Adams* (Boston: Houghton Mifflin, 1933).
5. Cited in Alasdair Clayre, *Work and Play* (New York: Harper & Row, 1975).
6. Simone Weil, op. cit.
7. Alasdair Clayre, op. cit.
8. Simone Weil, op. cit.

Chapter III:

1. Hugh J. Schonfield, *A History of Biblical Literature* (New York: Mentor Book, New American Library, 1962).
2. Luc Benoist, *Le Compagnonnage et les métiers*, in *Collection "Que Sais-je?"* (Paris: Presses Universitaires de France, 1970).

Chapter V:

1. Paracelsus, *Selected Writings of Paracelsus*, ed. Jolande Jacobi, Bollingen Series XXVIII (Princeton: Princeton University Press, 1951).

Chapter VII:

1. Walter Kerr, *The Decline of Pleasure* (New York: Simon & Schuster, 1962).
2. Henry James, *The Notebooks of Henry James*, ed. F. O. Matthiessen and Kenneth B. Murdock (New York: Oxford University Press, 1947).
3. Robert Capon, *Bed and Board* (New York: Simon & Schuster, 1965).
4. Simone Weil, op. cit.

Chapter X:

1. Emily Dickinson, *Complete Poems of Emily Dickinson*, ed. Thomas H. Johnson (Boston: Little, Brown, 1960).

Chapter XI:

1. Mircea Eliade, *The Forge and the Crucible: The Origins and Structures of Alchemy* (New York, Harper & Row, 1971).

2. Camara Laye, *L'Enfant Noir*, Paris, 1953, quoted in Titus Burckhardt, *Alchemy* (Baltimore: Penguin Books Inc., 1974).
3. Titus Burckhardt, ibid.
4. F. Sherwood Taylor, *The Alchemists* (St. Albans, Eng.: Paladin Paperbook, Granada, 1976).
5. Titus Burckhardt, op. cit.
6. Thomas Vaughan, *Lumen de Lumine*, ed. A. E. Waite (London, 1910).

Epilogue:
1. A. K. Coomaraswamy, op. cit.
2. Retold from the *Iliad*, Book XVIII.
3. Retold from "The Lost Words of Power" tr. John Martin Crawford, in Lin Carter, ed., *Dragons, Elves and Heroes* (New York: Ballantine, 1977).
4. Isha Schwaller de Lubicz, *Her-Bak*, Vol. 1: *The Living Face of Ancient Egypt*, tr. from the French by Charles Edgar Sprague (Baltimore: Penguin Books Inc., 1972; New York: Inner Traditions Press, 1977).
5. Lin Yutang, ed., *The Wisdom of China and India* (New York: Random House, 1942).
6. Chuang Tzü, in Robert O. Ballou, ed., *The Bible of the World* (New York: Viking Press, 1939).
7. Chuang Tzü, quoted in Thomas Merton, *The Way of Chuang Tzü* (New York: New Directions, 1969).
8. Martin Buber, ed., *Tales of the Hasidim, The Early Masters* (New York: Schocken Books, 1947).
9. Ibid.
10. Retold from an old folk tale.